# The New Faculty Career Guide

This hands-on resource supports the development of new faculty through a self-mentoring model, offering opportunities to reflect on and plan for teaching effectiveness, scholarship, and university and professional service.

Built on a foundation of collaboration and self-improvement, this book walks readers through the role of the college professor, covering a range of skills and responsibilities including developing course material, publishing journal articles, serving on committees, attending conferences, writing proposals for grants, and more. Each chapter features real-world case studies and mentoring moment activities for guided reflection.

Made eminently practical with sample CVs, tenure and promotion documentation, and syllabi, this guidebook is essential reading for prospective, first-year, and early-career faculty.

**Jodi Pilgrim** is Associate Dean and Professor in the College of Education at the University of Mary Hardin-Baylor, USA.

**Brenda Morton** is Director of the Doctor of Education program and Professor in the College of Education at the University of Mary Hardin-Baylor, USA, and Tallinn University, Estonia.

# The New Faculty Career Guide

## Self-Mentorship for Accelerated Growth and Development

Jodi Pilgrim and
Brenda Morton

NEW YORK AND LONDON

Designed cover image: Getty Images

First published 2026
by Routledge
605 Third Avenue, New York, NY 10158

and by Routledge
4 Park Square, Milton Park, Abingdon, Oxon, OX14 4RN

*Routledge is an imprint of the Taylor & Francis Group, an informa business*

© 2026 Jodi Pilgrim and Brenda Morton

The right of Jodi Pilgrim and Brenda Morton to be identified as authors of this work has been asserted in accordance with sections 77 and 78 of the Copyright, Designs and Patents Act 1988.

All rights reserved. The purchase of this copyright material confers the right on the purchasing institution to photocopy or download pages which bear the support material icon and a copyright line at the bottom of the page. No other parts of this book may be reprinted or reproduced or utilized in any form or by any electronic, mechanical, or other means, now known or hereafter invented, including photocopying and recording, or in any information storage or retrieval system, without permission in writing from the publishers.

*Trademark notice*: Product or corporate names may be trademarks or registered trademarks, and are used only for identification and explanation without intent to infringe.

ISBN: 978-1-032-77651-4 (hbk)
ISBN: 978-1-032-77256-1 (pbk)
ISBN: 978-1-003-48419-6 (ebk)

DOI: 10.4324/9781003484196

Typeset in Perpetua
by codeMantra

Access the Support Material: https://www.routledge.com/9781032772561

*This book is dedicated to our students, who aspire to share their knowledge and inspire the next generation as college professors.*

# Contents

List of Illustrations — xii
About the Authors — xiii
Preface — xv
Acknowledgements — xvi

**Introduction** — 1
- A Brief History  1
- Educational Capital  2
- Mentorship  3
- Faculty Focus  4
- Who?  5
- What?  6
- When?  7
- Where?  8
- Why?  8
- How?  9
- How to Use the Career Guide  11
- Mentoring Moments  11
- References  12

**PART I**
**Teaching Effectiveness** — 15

1. **What Is Teaching Effectiveness?** — 17
   - Faculty Focus  17
   - Introduction  17

CONTENTS

- The Challenges of Teaching In Higher Education  *18*
- The Basics  *21*
- High-Impact Practices  *24*
- Beyond the Basics  *25*
- Self-Mentorship  *29*
- References  *29*

2. **Preparing for Teaching Effectiveness**  33
    - Faculty Focus  *33*
    - Introduction  *33*
    - Implementing Your Teaching Philosophy  *34*
    - Planning  *39*
    - The Basics  *40*
    - Beyond the Basics: Planning for Class  *44*
    - Self-Mentorship  *46*
    - References  *46*

3. **Evaluating Teaching Effectiveness**  49
    - Faculty Focus  *49*
    - Introduction  *49*
    - Accountability and Assessment  *50*
    - The Role of Outcomes-Based Teaching, Learning, and Assessment  *50*
    - The Basics  *51*
    - Beyond the Basics  *55*
    - Self-Mentorship  *58*
    - References  *59*

**Mentoring Moments 1**  61
- Introduction: Exercise 0.1  *62*
- Introduction: Exercise 0.2  *63*
- Chapter 1: Exercise 1.1  *64*
- Chapter 1: Exercise 1.2  *65*
- Chapter 1: Exercise 1.3  *66*
- Chapter 2: Exercise 2.1  *67*
- Chapter 2: Exorcise 2.2  *68*
- Chapter 2: Exercise 2.3  *69*
- Chapter 3: Exercise 3.1  *70*
- Chapter 3: Exercise 3.2  *71*
- Chapter 3: Exercise 3.3  *72*

CONTENTS

**PART II**
**Research and Scholarship**      **75**

4. **What Is Scholarship?**      77
   - Faculty Focus   77
   - Introduction   77
   - Historical Perspective   78
   - Scholarship Reconsidered   79
   - Other Scholarly Activities   87
   - Scholarship and Professional Attainment: The Basics   87
   - Beyond the Basics   88
   - Self-Mentorship   89
   - References   89

5. **Planning and Engaging in Scholarship**      91
   - Faculty Focus   91
   - Introduction   91
   - Planning for Scholarship   92
   - Engaging in Scholarship   94
   - Creating Your Scholarly Identity   99
   - The Basics   104
   - Beyond the Basics   105
   - Self-Mentorship   105
   - References   105

6. **Tracking and Evaluating Scholarship**      107
   - Faculty Focus   107
   - Introduction   107
   - Scholarship Criteria   108
   - Evaluating Scholarly Productions   108
   - The Basics: Track Your Activities   110
   - Beyond the Basics: Self-Assessment and Peer Feedback   111
   - Self-Mentorship   115
   - References   116

**Mentoring Moments 2**      **117**
   - Chapter 4: Exercise 4.1   118
   - Chapter 4: Exercise 4.2   119
   - Chapter 4: Exercise 4.3   120

CONTENTS

- Chapter 5: Exercise 5.1   *121*
- Chapter 5: Exercise 5.2   *123*
- Chapter 5: Exercise 5.3   *124*
- Chapter 5: Exercise 5.4   *125*
- Chapter 5: Exercise 5.5   *132*
- Chapter 6: Exercise 6.1   *134*
- Chapter 6: Exercise 6.2   *135*
- Chapter 6: Exercise 6.3   *138*
- Chapter 6: Exercise 6.4   *139*
- Chapter 6: Exercise 6.5   *142*

## PART III
## Thriving in Academia — 143

### 7. University and Professional Service — 145
- Faculty Focus   *145*
- Introduction   *145*
- What Is University Service?   *146*
- What Is Professional Service?   *147*
- Planning for Service   *148*
- The Basics   *148*
- Beyond the Basics   *150*
- Self-Mentorship   *151*
- References   *151*

### 8. Faculty Evaluation — 153
- Faculty Focus   *153*
- Introduction   *154*
- Faculty Evaluation   *155*
- The Basics   *156*
- Beyond the Basics   *158*
- Self-Mentorship   *162*
- Reference   *162*

### 9. Thriving in Academia — 163
- Faculty Focus   *163*
- Introduction   *163*
- Academic Stressors   *164*
- Self-Care   *166*
- Self-Care Strategies for Faculty   *169*
- Implementing Your Self-Care Plan   *169*

- The Basics  *170*
- Beyond the Basics  *171*
- Self-Mentoring  *171*
- References  *171*

**Mentoring Moments 3**  173
- Chapter 7: Exercise 7.1  *174*
- Chapter 7: Exercise 7.2  *175*
- Chapter 7: Exercise 7.3  *176*
- Chapter 8: Exercise 8.1  *177*
- Chapter 9: Exercise 9.1  *178*
- Chapter 9: Exercise 9.2  *179*

*Index*  *183*

# Illustrations

**FIGURES**

| | | |
|---|---|---|
| Figure 1.1 | The TPACK Model | 27 |
| Figure 3.1 | AI-Generated Assignment and Rubric | 54 |
| Figure 6.1 | Assessment of Scholarship | 112 |

**TABLES**

| | | |
|---|---|---|
| Table 3.1 | Performance Assessment Examples | 52 |
| Table 5.1 | Writing Tools | 97 |
| Table 7.1 | Professional Service Examples | 148 |

# About the Authors

**Jodi Pilgrim** is an associate dean and professor at the University of Mary Hardin-Baylor (UMHB) in Belton, Texas. Jodi earned her bachelor's and master's degrees at Texas A&M University in College Station, Texas, and her doctorate in Reading Education at the University of North Texas. Jodi currently teaches literacy courses for undergraduate and graduate pre-service teachers. The faculty at UMHB selected her as the recipient of their Excellence in Teaching Award in 2014 and as the recipient of their Excellence in Scholarship Award in 2021. With over 25 years of experience in literacy education, Jodi's passion is ensuring striving readers receive the instruction and motivation necessary for success in the classroom. Jodi is a member of the International Society for Technology in Education (ISTE) as well as an ISTE certified educator. She is active in many state, national, and international professional organizations, including the Texas Association of Literacy Education (TALE). TALE awarded her the Texas Education Leadership in Literacy Award in 2019. Jodi's teaching and research interests include new/digital literacies, Universal Design for Learning, teacher preparation, and technology integration. Connect with Jodi on X @JLPilgrim

**Brenda Morton** is a professor and directs the doctor of education program at the University of Mary Hardin-Baylor (UMHB) in Belton, Texas. Brenda earned her bachelor's degree at Portland State University, her Master of Arts in Teaching, Doctor of Educational Leadership, and post-doc in trauma-response from George Fox University in Newberg, Oregon. She teaches research classes in the doctoral program, chairs dissertations, and teaches an undergraduate trauma class. Brenda is a highly regarded international leader in the field of trauma and trauma-informed instruction. Her research focuses on trauma, at-risk youth, foster children, and inclusionary practices. Brenda is also a Fulbright Scholar and Fulbright Specialist, both to Estonia, where she continues to serve as a faculty member at Tallinn University. In 2024, she was selected as the recipient of the Excellence in Scholarship

## ABOUT THE AUTHORS

Award from UMHB. Brenda authored the book *Braving the Dark: Surviving Foster Care,* which shares the accounts of those pursuing post-secondary education who lived in foster care. She co-authored *Trauma-Informed School Practices: Building Expertise to Transform Schools,* a guide for P-12 schools looking to transition to a trauma-informed model of education.

# Preface

Having navigated the promotion and tenure process ourselves, we understand that it can feel like assembling a puzzle without a clear picture of the final product. As educators, we are committed to sharing what we have learned about teaching effectiveness, scholarship, and university service to support your growth and development as a new faculty member. This career guide is a product of that commitment. It was originally conceived as part of our thoughtful planning for a course in our education doctoral program, *The American College and University Professor*, at UMHB. As we designed the class, we identified a gap in resources—one that not only conveyed essential knowledge, but also provided practical tools to scaffold learning and planning processes.

Our goal is to create a resource that equips new and/or future faculty members with opportunities to engage deeply with the material, apply concepts meaningfully, and reflect on their professional journey. In this book, we have combined research, real-world examples, and reflective activities, and we hope it will serve as a guide for aspiring educators and scholars seeking to develop the skills, strategies, and insights necessary for success. Each chapter of this text represents a piece of the academic puzzle, with Faculty Focus scenarios and Mentoring Moments to promote self-reflection and self-mentorship of your professional practices.

Between us, we have been honored with an Excellence in Teaching award and two Excellence in Scholarship awards. The honors did not come early in our careers – it took significant work to plan, implement, and assesses our professional practices. We share strategies we used as we navigated the world of higher education. You will encounter themes of "planning, engaging, and assessing" as you work through this text. Our intent is that when you reach the chapter on the tenure and promotion process, the completed puzzle of academia will have been revealed, equipping you to begin a successful career in academia. We are grateful for the support and resources that have helped shape our careers, and we are excited to share our knowledge and experiences with you. We look forward to the impact this resource may have on your growth as an educator and scholar.

# Acknowledgements

As professors, we thank our university for the support we received during the tenure and promotion process. We are fortunate to have had clear expectations and guidelines as well as support through the Center for Excellence in Learning and Teaching. As colleagues, we thank current and past associates who modeled excellence in teaching, scholarship, and service. We appreciate your friendship. As teachers, we thank the students who inspired this book. We look forward to seeing current and future learners progress towards their career goals. As authors, we thank our editors, Alex and Kyanna, for their patience and guidance. Finally, as busy wives, with limited spare time for household responsibilities, we thank our spouses, Michael and Dave, who support us through long hours and crazy schedules.

# Introduction

The academic experience at colleges and universities provides students with the opportunity to learn and apply practical information about a future professional career to increase their understanding of a specific discipline. This opportunity costs on average $36,436 per year in the United States, including tuition, books, supplies, fees, and living expenses (Hanson, 2023). What role does the college professor play in students' academic experiences? The purpose of this introductory chapter is to provide an overview of the role of the professorship and to describe how to utilize the Faculty Career Guide for self-mentorship and accelerated growth.

## A BRIEF HISTORY

Just as a singer is a person who sings, a professor, according to the term's Latin origin, is a person who professes (Merriam-Webster, n.d.). A professor is considered to be an expert in their field, which is why the role of a professor has traditionally been viewed as a high-ranking/prominent position within educational institutions like colleges and universities. Just as finances govern educational institutions today, financially related staff shortages were a problem in medieval Europe. Universities needed teachers, of course, but scholars often rejected teaching because there was little to gain financially (University of Leeds, 2023a). Efforts to secure funding for lecturers were documented in 1432 (University of Leeds, 2023a), and most early positions, eventually referred to as professorships, were endowed, meaning gifts from wealthy patrons provided stipends for the teaching posts.

The history of the title of *professor* evolved from these endowed chairs and began in medieval Europe during the Tudor period (University of Leeds, 2023b). Initially referred to as lectureships or readerships, the title evolved to professorships through a "gradually developing hierarchy of teachers" (University of Leeds, 2023b, para. 1). The "professor" became top of the hierarchy in the 1540s when Henry VIII created endowed teachers (or chairs), or "King's Professors" (para. 3).

DOI: 10.4324/9781003484196-1

The term professor eventually referred to the holders of salaried or endowed teaching offices, or to the highest class of these. Titles such as reader, lecturer, instructor, and tutor, were given to teachers of lower rank.

This abbreviated history lesson presents two important ideas. First, it communicates how the title of professor rose in rank above the other university teachers, like tutors, lecturers, and readers. Second, it provides insight into the original and primary role of the professor, which involved teaching, and "professing" expertise (Evans, 2016, p. 22; University of Leeds, 2023c, para. 1). Teaching is key to the role of the professor and is the focus of the next two chapters.

In addition to teaching, research and writing developed from the responsibility of professing, not just to university students, but to the general public. Experts can share knowledge orally, through lecture. However, disseminating information through the written word became another way to teach (University of Leeds, 2023c). Much of the initial writing by scholars was religious in nature and was a way to expand the church.

Higher education in the U.S. also has a unique story. Harvard University, founded in 1636, claims to be the first institution of higher education in the U.S. (Cipriano, S., 2019). Over time, institutions like Harvard began to train more men for different kinds of careers (Education Writers Association, 2021). Harvard College's first commencement took place in 1642, in which nine men graduated. The college curriculum generally remained classical and narrow until the 19th century when the model of higher education evolved, probably due to a need for increased knowledge in the sciences, which could improve the manufacturing of such products as steel and petroleum (Education Writers Association, 2021). As colleges evolved into universities that granted doctoral degrees in specific areas of study, the concept of the research university evolved (Fischman and Gardner, 2022).

## EDUCATIONAL CAPITAL

The expertise yielded by a professor should expand beyond a knowledge base to include experience and practice within a field or domain. Common sense tells us that someone studying to be a teacher would want to be taught by someone with experience in this role, just as an individual studying to be a nurse would expect instruction from an experienced practitioner. Professors with real world experience understand the specific skills needed for jobs. Therefore, professors should have professional experience in their field of study.

Today, because of their expertise, professors engage in advanced research and share their knowledge and experience with students through their teaching responsibilities. The role of the professor extends to contributing to the academic community through research and publishing. Professors have an opportunity to shape the intellectual and professional development of students as they foster skills required in their discipline. As professors ourselves, we prefer this broad description of a professor over the narrow one provided by the U.S. Bureau of Labor Statistics, which refers to the college professor as a postsecondary teacher: "Postsecondary Teachers" instruct students in a variety of academic subjects beyond the high school level" (U.S. Bureau of Labor Statistics, 2023, para. 1). The same source states that

> the educational requirements for this job vary by subject and the type of educational institution, but that typically, postsecondary teachers must have a Ph.D. However, a master's degree may be enough for some postsecondary teachers at community colleges, and others may need work experience in their field of expertise (U.S. Bureau of Labor Statistics, 2023).

Even though this job description is not *inaccurate*, it certainly does not capture the entirety of what it takes or what is required of a college/university professor. According to Evans (2016), "professorship has become something of an enigma. It is 'a slippery term.'" (p. 1). Evans, a UK professor, shares that the historic interpretation of professorship in the UK is focused on a record of accomplishments, rather than a role to be carried out. She expresses concern regarding this observation since the role of a professor is more than in name only. Tenure-track professors must earn the respect and the title, even after a job is secured.

## MENTORSHIP

Earning an advanced degree is only the beginning of the path to success as a professor in higher education. The process of tenure and promotion requires ongoing growth, adaptability, and a clear understanding of institutional expectations. The purpose of this book is to make the expectations and path to success as clear as possible. Just as a mentee learns from the counsel of a wise friend or teacher, our intent is that our readers grow using our self-mentorship model, in which we support new faculty in their roles in higher education through information, examples, self-reflection, and guiding activities.

The concept of mentoring can be traced to a character in Homer's *The Odyssey* (Simon et al., 2003). The character, named Mentor, was a trusted friend of Odysseus, who was tasked with looking after Odysseus' household in his absence. Through the voice and image of Mentor, the Greek goddess Athena intervened during a tough time for Telemachus, the son of Odysseus, and provided the support and guidance he needed. A mentor can reflect the voice of experience. The Merriam-Webster dictionary (n.d.) presents a modern-day definition of mentor as "a trusted counsellor or guide." As mentors, we will share a variety of experiences we have witnessed related to the growth of faculty during the tenure and promotion process. For example, in our chapter about scholarship, we will share ways to develop a research agenda. We also focus on the ins and outs of a professor's daily schedule. These scenarios, found at the beginning of each chapter, are referred to as "Faculty Focus." We include these intentional prompts to encourage our readers to reflect on failures and successes of potential colleagues and to make personal connections with the goal of self-growth and improvement. The following scenario is our first Faculty Focus, which we share now as we transition to the role of the modern professorship.

## FACULTY FOCUS

> *Adriana was frustrated. A junior in Dr. Longoria's class, she was confused about an upcoming assignment. Even though the assignment description was available on the course syllabus, Adriana wanted to confirm the connections she was making between the assignment and the content covered in class. She had visited her professor's office that morning to ask questions, but Dr. Longoria was not yet in for the day. It seemed her professor was rarely on campus. Adriana checked the door and noticed that Dr. Longoria's office hours started at 1 p.m. Returning at 1 p.m., Adriana was disappointed to see Dr. Longoria's door shut. Even though the office light was on, Dr. Longoria was not there. Adriana decided to wait around for a while. In the meantime, she sent an email message to Dr Longoria, who was typically good about responding to emails promptly. After another hour of waiting, with no email response, Adriana grew even more frustrated. Finally, Dr. Longoria arrived and welcomed Adriana into her office with a smile. Adriana got her questions answered, and her temperament eventually improved.*

At first glance, it may seem as if Dr. Longoria's presence on campus is lacking. What Adriana did not realize was that Dr. Longoria was serving on a Search Committee that had a candidate on campus for an interview during Dr. Longoria's office hours. Adriana also did not realize that Dr. Longoria's office hours began at 1 p.m. on the day she was looking for her because she supports her students in the field each morning. Finally, Adriana was likely to have no idea that at the end of the day, Dr. Longoria would head home and continue grading online submissions later that night.

One take-away from this mentoring moment is that the role of the professor is not always visible to others. Professors have many responsibilities that extend beyond the role of teacher. Other take-aways from this scenario highlight Dr. Longoria's successes. Dr. Longoria had her office hours posted for her students, which is a basic expectation. Dr. Longoria is known for responding to emails in a prompt manner. Dr. Longoria greets her students with a smile. Dr. Longoria's syllabus included a description of the assignment in question, and the assignment was leading Adriana to make connections to content learned in class. Adriana was learning!

One tip we might have suggested for Dr. Longoria would be to have a note ready to post on her door for instances like this moment where she had to miss office hours. Unfortunately, this one instance of missing office hours may have affected Adriana's overall view of her professor's availability to students. Availability to students is an area in which professors are evaluated when it comes to teaching effectiveness. Using the *Who, What, When, Where, and Why* framework, we next describe the role of the college professor. Continue to reflect on Dr. Longoria's day as we elaborate on the professorship using the Five W's Framework.

## WHO?

Who becomes a college professor? According to the Princeton Review (2025), "this profession is thus best suited for motivated self-starters, and its highest rewards [tenure] are given to those who can identify and explore original problems in their fields" (para. 1). Because tenured professors have relatively high job security and professional freedom (Princeton Review, 2023), tenure is the goal of most individuals aspiring to teach in higher education. Tenured professors have earned a position of stature at their university, having successfully navigated the tenure process, which requires them to achieve rigorous standards in the areas of teaching, scholarship, and service. However, a trend in higher education is to hire part-time, non-tenure-track faculty as a way to save money. For instance, in the fall of 2021, of the 1.5 million faculty at degree-granting postsecondary institutions, 56 percent were full-time and 44 percent were part-time. According to an article in *Inside Higher Education*, colleges and universities of all kinds are increasingly relying on non-tenure-track faculty members. "Since adjuncts are paid less than those on the tenure track (and frequently lack benefits), it costs colleges less to have a section taught by an adjunct than by someone who is tenured or on the tenure track" (Jaschik, 2023, para. 1). The key is that at a minimum, institutions of higher education must provide quality education; therefore, they must meet the Higher Learning Commission's (HLC) criteria for accreditation and assumed practices. For more information on criteria, visit https://download.hlcommission.org/FacultyGuidelines_OPB.pdf.

Faculty include professors, associate professors, assistant professors, instructors, lecturers, clinical professors, assisting professors, adjunct professors, and interim professors. For the purposes of this book, we use the term "college professor" for individuals who have earned a tenure-track position and will be moving through the ranks from assistant professor, to associate professor, to full professor. As described by Alicita Rodriguez (2020), the basic progression of rank starts at assistant professor. Assistant professors can move up to the rank of associate professor—promotion timeline varies across universities. Finally, the highest of the three ranks is full professor.

As previously mentioned, the educational requirements for this job vary by subject and the type of educational institution, but typically, postsecondary teachers must have a Ph.D. or a terminal degree in their discipline. For instance, a Doctor of Education, an Ed.D., is a terminal degree. The culminating activity for these degrees, the dissertation, demonstrates intelligence, command of the relevant academic literature, and application of methodological rigor (Gasman, 2021). In addition to a degree and a dissertation, some jobs may expect the applicant for a tenure-track position to already have begun "professing" knowledge in a discipline through scholarly writing and publishing.

## WHAT?

What is the role of the college professor? Again, this question is the focus of the entire book, but for the purpose of this section, let's review the role wholistically. The role, not often explicitly defined (Evans, 2016), includes a broad range of responsibilities. We briefly outline the responsibilities here but subsequently explore these responsibilities throughout our book.

## Responsibilities

### Teacher/Practitioner

We concur with other scholars that teaching is the primary responsibility of the professor (Kezar and Maxey, 2016; Seldin, 2004; Seldin and Miller, 2009). In addition to knowledge of one's content, teaching requires knowledge of pedagogical practices. Furthermore, teaching goes hand in hand with the other responsibilities. For example, how can college professors teach well if they are not maintaining expertise in their field, and what better way to maintain expertise in their field than to conduct relevant research?

Teaching responsibilities vary depending on the institution. For example, we work at a teaching institution, and our course load is 12 credit hours per semester. Teaching load varies based on many factors, including institutional type, discipline, research/grant responsibilities, etc. Teaching responsibilities include the development of curricula, preparing syllabi and lessons, grading, evaluating student progress, maintaining the learning management system (LMS), and more. Additionally, in the 21st century, teaching responsibilities also include the ability to provide instruction in a remote setting.

### Mentor/Advisor

A faculty member may be a mentor for a colleague, offering support for the purpose of furthering their career. In addition, faculty members are considered advisors to students. A professor may engage with a student in a variety of ways to offer support and guidance in academics and career exploration. The role can be both unofficial and official, in terms of responsibilities. Many universities have personnel hired specifically for advising purposes. At our university, we advise our undergraduate and graduate students in their degree plan progress.

### Scholar

Scholarly attainment leads to a faculty position and helps one maintain a tenure-track position. Faculty roles typically include researching, writing, and presenting in a field of study. The research does not stop once a degree is obtained. In order to maintain expertise in a quickly changing world, one must continue a research agenda. We consider the scholar to be a continuing learner that engages in professional growth. At some universities, scholars must possess the skills to generate external funding to support their work.

## Academic Leader

In a study of over 1,000 professorial questionnaire respondents in which participants were asked about the purpose of the professor, responses indicated strong support for an academic leadership role, particularly within the university (Evans, 2016). Within the academic community, professors engage in leadership roles by participating in departmental meetings, serving on committees, and contributing to institutional decision-making. In addition, they often collaborate with colleagues to develop curricula, academic policies, and effective learning experiences. These are all examples of university service. Professors also engage in professional service by reviewing research papers, serving as conference organizers, and sharing their expertise with peers.

## Colleague

Kezar and Maxey (2016) present collegiality as an element of all types of faculty work. They assert that faculty members must express mutual respect and civility:

> Collegiality can also be nurtured by such practical strategies as finding appropriate ways—commensurate with their appointment types—to include the diverse range of faculty members in institutional governance including faculty senates and advisory groups and, where appropriate, search committees . . . cultivating and conveying collegiality should be an ongoing, dynamic characteristic of a university or college. (Page 71)

What does this look like? Perhaps it is an "all of the above" category. When we teach, we respect our students and our co-workers. When we research and participate in organizations relevant to our field, we respect one another. When we serve as mentors for our colleagues, we do so respectfully, without judgment.

## WHEN?

Depending on the university of employment, many tenure-track professors hold nine-month contracts. Summer teaching is optional in many cases. Professors often manage their own schedules based on their course schedules, department and university meetings, time spent on emails/correspondence, and selected office or clinic hours. However, professors work long days, both on and off campus. In a study of workloads at Boise State University (Flaherty, 2014), preliminary findings indicated that faculty at his university worked 61 hours per week and that senior faculty worked slightly longer hours than junior faculty.

## WHERE?

Job opportunities for the general professor include positions at private, public, and community colleges. Most professors spend most of their time teaching, but instruction does not always occur in a physical classroom setting. Remote teaching has become just as common, and as necessary, as face-to-face (f2f) teaching. In the 21st century, there has been a massive expansion of online higher education. According to a *New York Times* article, about a third of higher education coursework was entirely online before 2020 (Marcus, 2022). Covid-19 shutdowns increased online offerings. This same article also reported that faculty favoured hybrid classes, in which they combined online with f2f instruction.

## WHY?

Why become a college professor? One reason for pursuing a tenure-track position may be that tenured professors have relatively high job security and professional freedom. Overall, though, the answer to this question varies, of course. The answer is not always based on opportunities for a higher income. For example, business professionals typically make more in the real world than they do in higher education. Principals and superintendents make more money in the K-12 setting than they do in higher education. Nurses and other health care practitioners make more as clinicians than professors. Then why become a professor? We guess the answer for many reflects a passion for their field and the desire to make a difference. We share our own stories as examples.

### Brenda's *Why*

*I was contacted by my former Master of Arts (MAT) in Teaching cohort leader. She was looking for a high school English teacher willing to mentor a student teacher for the upcoming school year. I jumped at the opportunity. I remembered how much I learned from my mentors and hoped to give my student teacher a great experience. The year seemed to fly by. At the end of her time with me, I realized how much I enjoyed mentoring and called the university to let them know I would be happy to take another student teacher in the future. About two weeks later, my former cohort leader contacted me again about a faculty position that had opened in the MAT program. I enjoyed teaching at the high school level and had not considered becoming a professor. Yet, the more we discussed the position, the more I knew I wanted to apply. My "why" was the opportunity to prepare teachers for the classroom. What if I could* help develop high-quality teachers for the classroom? What would it be like to mentor an entire cohort each year? I was hired a couple of months later. Over the last 15 years, I have had the privilege of working with pre-service teachers, master's, and doctoral students and serving in several leadership positions in the College of Education.

## Jodi's Why

My initial desire to "teach teachers" began when I was an undergraduate student. As many educators who have family members in the teaching profession, I was supressing my calling. My mom and aunts were teachers, and I resisted entering the profession because it seemed to be a lot of work for a job that few appreciated. As a nerdy college student who enjoyed learning, I would take a class and love that subject, whether it was geography, history, English.... I changed my major a lot. Well, I thought, teachers get to teach all subjects! I finally decided to try taking education classes to see what it was about. I LOVED the content related to pedagogy, and I loved my professors' teaching styles. They taught their classes unlike any other professors at the university—later I realize they were modelling effective K12 teaching practices. Children's Literature was a course I found especially inspirational. I was an avid reader as a child, and as I became reacquainted with the genres I read in elementary school, I began getting excited about the ways I could use literature in the classroom.

I made my last degree plan change as an undergraduate, and my appreciation for my undergraduate professors continued to grow. Their skill in modelling effective teaching practices contributed to my thoughts of one day "teaching teachers." When I started teaching elementary school, I had a particular passion for my striving readers. Every degree I earned after my bachelor's degree was focused on literacy instruction, which students of all ages and across all content areas need. I enjoyed teaching elementary and middle school students. Now, as a professor, I enjoy sharing my passions and modelling effective instructional practices for my college students. In addition, I know that for each teacher I train, the impact on children's lives grows!

## HOW?

How does a tenure-track position work? The puzzle behind earning a tenure and promotion is all in HOW you build your portfolio. Keep in mind that we've already mentioned that the role of the faculty member and the future of tenure-track positions is shifting. However, it is unlikely that the evaluation of faculty members will change quickly over the next few years. Historically, faculty members must demonstrate effective performance in the areas of teaching, research, and service. Teaching universities, which are student-centered in nature, require a greater emphasis on the role of teaching. For example, at our university, teaching effectiveness makes up 60 percent of our faculty evaluation. We also have a greater teaching load than research-oriented universities. The expectation is that we teach a 12-hour load, where a different professor at another university may teach just six or nine hours a semester, with the expectation that the remaining time is spent on research and writing. Regardless, the faculty member's performance in these areas is important. The career guide is divided into three parts based on these three areas.

## Part I: Teaching Effectiveness

Student learning is the priority of all institutions of higher education and is directly related to teaching effectiveness (Kezar & Maxey, 2016). Faculty are required to provide evidence of quality classroom teaching (Seldin, 2004). When considering evidence of teaching effectiveness, faculty need to be reflective and intentional in improving teaching based on student success as well as student evaluations. One needs to consider teaching philosophies, objectives teaching methods, curricula revisions, and syllabi. Evaluating teaching effectiveness is a challenge all universities face.

> Chapter 1—What is Teaching Effectiveness?
> Chapter 2—Preparing for Teaching Effectiveness
> Chapter 3—Assessing Teaching Effectiveness

## Part II: Research and Scholarship

Faculty are expected to maintain a scholarly presence in their field. They are also required to provide evidence of scholarly attainment. The level of attainment varies from university to university and should focus on how research supports the discipline as well as the mission of the department or institution (Seldin and Miller, 2009).

> Chapter 4—What is Scholarship?
> Chapter 5—Planning and Engaging in Scholarship
> Chapter 6—Tracking and Evaluating Scholarship

## Part III: Thriving in Academia

There are many ways to thrive in academia. Even though colleges and universities generally recognize some kind of institutional service as a role of a faculty member, it is also a way to use your knowledge and skills to help the community and to thrive in your profession. Service is typically considered less important than teaching or research in terms of the tenure process. Regardless of the weight placed on this faculty role, documenting university service is important, as it highlights one's contribution to a college or university. It can also be reflective of one's ability to collaborate and be collegial as we as thrive in academia.

Chapter 7—University and Professional Service
Chapter 8—Faculty Evaluation
Chapter 9—Thriving in the Academy

## HOW TO USE THE CAREER GUIDE

We spend the rest of this book providing details about how to develop teaching, research, and service as a means to obtaining tenure and rank. Our intended audience encompasses new faculty members across all disciplines. Our expertise in education may limit our content knowledge across disciplines, so we draw on our knowledge of best practices and our experiences in higher education. As full professors who have experienced the promotion and tenure process, we share both successes and failures as a way to demonstrate growth through self-reflection. With each chapter in this unique text, we offer the foundations for success.

## MENTORING MOMENTS

Each chapter concludes by providing mentorship for you and your journey, connecting ideas from the chapter to exercises at the end of each part of the textbook, called Mentoring Moments. We use Mentoring Moments as a means of self-mentorship. Personal growth and improvement require action on the part of the new faculty member to be an active agent in the process. Therefore, we encourage self-mentorship, which involves "cultivating your own professional growth through reflection, networking, and seeking out appropriate resources" (Bloom, 2007, p. 56). Reflective practitioners exhibit self-awareness—they understand their strengths and weaknesses and monitor and adjust their professional performance (Bloom, 2007). In addition to self-assessment and reflection of current practices, concrete application of new knowledge and resources represents a critical component of self-mentorship. In order to attain our goals, which may include the achievement of tenure and promotion, we support self-mentorship through a variety of exercises, developed specifically to accelerate growth of the new faculty member. These exercises, called mentoring moments, are compiled within Parts I, II, and III of this textbook. Mentoring Moment's exercises help build the skills necessary to excel at teaching, scholarship, and service.

Part I: Chapter 1-3 Exercises
Part II: Chapter 4-6 Exercises
Part III: Chapters 7-9 Exercises

## Next Steps

Next step(s) for the reader are to work through Exercises 0.1 and 0.2 prior to beginning Part I of the book. In the first exercise, you will reflect on your "why."

In Exercise 0.2, you will complete a traditional KWL chart, in which you will brainstorm everything you know about the following roles of the professor in your discipline: Teaching excellence, scholarship, and service. Next, in the W column, list the questions you have about each of these areas of focus. In other words, what do you Want (W) to know about each of these topics? As you read Parts I-III of the book, you will revisit the chart's L (Learned) column to add things you have learned about earning tenure and promotion.

## REFERENCES

Bloom, P. J. (2007). Becoming a self-mentor. *Exchange, the Early Leader's Magazine*, p. 54–57. https://fpg.unc.edu/sites/fpg.unc.edu/files/resources/presentations-and-webinars/Becoming-a-Self-Mentor.pdf

Cipriano, S. (2019). Harvard 1642: America's first commencement. We're History. https://werehistory.org/harvard-1642-americas-first-commencement/#:~:text=Harvard's%20first%20commencement%20was%20a,Tobias%20Barnard%2C%20and%20Nathaniel%20Brewster

Education Writers Association. (2021). History and background: College faculty & staff. https://ewa.org/issues/higher-ed/college-faculty-staff-history-background

Evans, L. (2016). The purpose of professors: professionalism, pressures, and performance. Stimulus Paper. *Leadership Foundation for Higher Education*. file:///C:/Users/jpilgrim/Downloads/publishedversion.pdf

Flaherty, C. (2014). So much to do, so little time. *Inside Higher Ed*. https://www.insidehighered.com/news/2014/04/09/research-shows-professors-work-long-hours-and-spend-much-day-meetings

Fischman, W., & Gardner, H. (2022). *The real world of college: What higher education is and what it can be*. The MIT Press.

Gasman, M. (2021). *Candid advice for new faculty members: A guide to getting tenure and advancing your academic career*. Myers Education Press.

Hanson, M. (2023). Average cost of college & tuition. Education Data Initiative. https://educationdata.org/average-cost-of-college#:~:text=The%20average%20cost%20of%20college,over%20the%20past%2010%20years

Jaschik, S. (2017). When Colleges Rely on Adjuncts, Where Does the Money Go? *Inside Higher Education*. https://www.insidehighered.com/news/2017/01/05/study-looks-impact-adjunct-hiring-college-spending-patterns#:~:text=And%20administrators%20frequently%20defend%20their,or%20on%20the%20tenure%20track

Kezar, A., & Maxey, D. (2016). Envisioning the faculty for the 21st century: Moving to a mission-oriented and learner-centered model. Rutgers University Press.

Marcus, J. (2022). With online learning, 'Let's take a breath and see what worked and didn't work'. *The New York Times*. https://www.nytimes.com/2022/10/06/education/learning/online-learning-higher-education.html

Merriam-Webster. (n.d.). Professor. In Merriam-Webster.com dictionary. https://www.merriam-webster.com/dictionary/professor

Rodriguez, A. (2020). Professor—What's in a title? *CU Denver News.* https://news.ucdenver.edu/professor/

Seldin, P. (2004). *Teaching portfolio: A practical guide to improved performance and promotion/tenure decisions.* Anker Publishing Company, Inc.

Seldin, P., & Miller, J. E. (2009). *The academic portfolio: A practical guide to documenting teaching, research, and service.* Jossey-Bass: A Wiley Imprint.

Simon, C. J., Bloxham, L., Doyle, D., Haily, M., Hawks, J. H., Light, K., Scibilia, D. P., & Simmons, E. (2003). *Mentoring for mission: Nurturing new faculty at church-related colleges.* William B. Eerdmans Publishing Company.

The Princeton Review. (2025). Professor. https://www.princetonreview.com/careers/127/professor

U.S. Bureau of Labor Statistics. (2023). Occupational outlook handbook: Postsecondary teachers. https://www.bls.gov/ooh/education-training-and-library/postsecondary-teachers.htm?cmgfrm=?cmgfrm

University of Leeds. (2023a). What is a Professor?: How did professorships come about? https://professors.leeds.ac.uk/what-is-a-professor/when-did-the-title-professor-first-start-to-be-used/

University of Leeds. (2023b). What is a Professor?: When did the title 'professor' first start to be used? https://professors.leeds.ac.uk/what-is-a-professor/when-did-the-title-professor-first-start-to-be-used/

University of Leeds. (2023c). What is a Professor?: How has professorship evolved over the centuries? https://professors.leeds.ac.uk/what-is-a-professor/when-did-the-title-professor-first-start-to-be-used/

# Part I
# Teaching Effectiveness

Chapter 1

# What Is Teaching Effectiveness?

## FACULTY FOCUS

*Dr. Santos, a recent doctoral graduate in Sociology, has just been hired as an assistant professor at a mid-sized university. Although he is excited to begin teaching, this is his first time leading undergraduate courses, and the idea of stepping into a classroom as the instructor feels both thrilling and daunting. He will be teaching two face-to-face introductory sociology courses and one online upper-level course on social stratification.*

*Dr. Santos finds himself contemplating the question: What does it mean to be an effective teacher? Reflecting on his own experiences as a college student, he remembers professors who led thought-provoking discussions and those who could explain complex theories with clarity and relevance. He also recalls long, monotonous lectures where students were disengaged or unsure how the material applied to the real world. How can he relate to GenZ students? He never took an online course, so teaching effectively in an online environment is also hard to imagine.*

## INTRODUCTION

Simply stated, good teaching is important. In this chapter, we address the definition(s) of teaching effectiveness from a higher education perspective. We also consider aspects of teaching that have evolved in the 21st century due to advances in technology and online learning. Teaching effectiveness in an online environment looks different than teaching effectiveness in a face-to-face (f2f) classroom. Describing teaching effectiveness is no easy task, as it involves complexities far greater than the effective delivery of content knowledge. Teaching effectiveness involves the knowledge of the learning processes as well as the preparation of teaching, treatment of students, and the assessment of student outcomes (Bain, 2004). Dr. Santos is experiencing an unease that many new faculty encounter as they become "teacher" for the first time. Developing coursework has not always been a component of graduate coursework leading to roles in higher education. College and university professors often learn the art of teaching and classroom management on the job as they continue to teach classes year after year (Buller, 2010; Hettiarachchy, 2021).

Many institutions, including our own, have revised doctoral programs to include a focus on effective ways to teach in one's discipline. In addition, colleges and universities have expanded faculty orientation programs to include professional development programs. Centers for teaching and learning have been developed to provide advanced training for professors to enable success in the tenure and promotion process (Buller, 2010). With student success a priority, knowledge about effective teaching cannot wait. Subject matter expertise comprises only part of teaching. The purpose of this chapter is to address the need for intentional focus on pedagogy. This chapter begins with an overview of *why* the professor should focus on teaching effectiveness in terms of student success. We then transition to the basics of teaching effectiveness and learning processes.

## THE CHALLENGES OF TEACHING IN HIGHER EDUCATION

In our introductory chapter, we shared a brief narrative of the history of colleges and universities. Another aspect of this narrative that we have yet to address relates to the historically elite nature of institutions of higher education. For centuries, higher education in college and university settings was for privileged individuals. Initially, the elite included primarily male students as well as the dominant racial or ethnic group in control of society at that time. Religious domination also impacted access to knowledge (Soliday and Lombardi, 2018). Historical events, such as the Enlightenment in the late 1600s and early 1700s, as well as the Democratic age, beginning with the American, French, and later European revolutions of the 19th century, challenged this reality (Soliday and Lombardi, 2018). Access to higher education increased in America during the post World War II era with the advent of the GI bill. Lyndon Johnson's Great Society programs, which sought to eliminate poverty and racial injustice, provided educational opportunities to those with previously limited access, through Pell grants and Perkins loans. These programs, which expanded admissions and increased affordability over time, boosted college enrollment among high school graduates from roughly 40% in 1960 to over 65% by 2000 (Soliday and Lombardi, 2018).

Among the successes of US education is the increase in diverse student populations. Within the last 15–20 years, college readiness for all students has become a priority across the US (Brint, 2018). The Common Core State Standards Initiative (CCSSI) (2010), established to outline standards for what students should know at the end of each grade (K-12) and to ensure skills and readiness necessary for college, work, and life success, reflected a nationwide effort to increase academic rigor.

The Every Student Succeeds Act (2015) further advanced equity by requiring the high academic standards needed for success in college and careers (Brint, 2018; US Dept of Education, n.d.). About two thirds of high school graduates enroll in college right after high school (Soliday and Lombardi, 2018). Opportunities to attend college have expanded, enabling upward mobility for all students (Brint, 2018).

With this success come challenges, as professors seek to support *all* students. According to a report of 5706 institutions by the National Center for Education, the full-time retention rate for students in postsecondary institutions was 76.5% in the fall of 2022 (National Center for Education Statistics, 2022). Unfortunately, the completion rate for Black and Hispanic students is much lower than for White and Asian students (Soliday, and Lombardi, 2018). Addressing issues of opportunity and inclusion is a priority.

Another pressing issue colleges and universities face is the rise of mental health issues. The mental health of children and youth, especially those impacted by trauma, has become a public health issue (Vostanis, 2017). As early as 2013, the numbers of young people impacted by trauma began reaching epidemic levels (Blaustein, 2013). Before COVID-19, it was reported that more than 50% of children experienced adverse childhood events before the age of 18 (Centers for Disease Control, 2015). While mental health providers have known about the significance of traumatic events, knowledge of the Adverse Childhood Experiences (ACEs) survey is new to the field of education. It was only within the last 5–7 years that educators began to engage with the ACEs survey, which highlighted the link between trauma, academic and social development, and long-term life outcomes. Before the widespread introduction of the survey, educators may have recognized that some students struggled in school, but they lacked a clear understanding of how trauma specifically impacted academic and social functioning.

Berardi & Morton (2019) defined trauma as "a term to describe the aftermath or impact of an event, whether real or perceived, that interrupts a person's ability to maintain a sense of psychological and/or physical safety and well-being" (p. 14). Simply put, trauma damages the brain (Berardi & Morton, 2019; Morton, 2018). This trauma results in disrupted neurodevelopment, including social, emotional, and cognitive impairment, adoption of health-risk behaviors, disease, disability, social problems, and early death (Feletti, et al., 1998). As a student attempts to engage in the learning environment, the consistent production of norepinephrine, due to heightened anxiety, triggers a fight-flight-freeze response (Everly & Lating, 2012; van der Kolk, 2014; Vermetten & Bremner, 2002). The student encounters triggering situations and events during the day, resulting in heightened awareness of their surroundings. This causes the student to engage in an ongoing safety assessment for signs or sounds of danger, causing an inability to focus on academic material or to engage in self-regulation, often resulting in unpredictable, impulsive, or otherwise inappropriate behaviors (Carrion & Wong, 2012; Perry, 2006; Souers & Hall, 2016).

The fields of traumatology and neurobiology continue to advance our understanding of the impact of trauma. In connection with the ACEs survey, we have confirmation of the detrimental impact of stress and trauma on both psychosocial and physical health (Berardi & Morton, 2019). With this knowledge, educators must reassess and reevaluate the traditional model of teaching in learning in schools, as it is not effective in meeting the needs of the overwhelming majority of students today (Berardi & Morton, 2019).

Fischman and Gardner (2022) explored the views of thousands of students and campus personnel and reported that 66% of on-campus adults ranked mental health as the most important problem on campuses. Their work occurred prior to the onset of the COVID-19 pandemic. Since the pandemic, rates of anxiety, depression and suicidal ideation on college campuses have increased (Flannery, 2023). Students attending higher education institutions come to campus with complex needs, and an awareness of trends is important, as faculty may observe some of the behaviors caused by stress and anxiety. While campuses have increased services for students, there has not been training for professors (Soliday & Lombardi, 2018).

Post-COVID trends also include a drop in college attendance among undergraduates of almost 10% (Fischer, 2022). There are no definitive answers for the drop in enrollment, but Fischer (2022) suggests that it could be a result of generational trends. The Pew Research Center measures public attitudes, focusing on differences in key issues and attitudes across demographic groups, and categorizes individuals who were born at similar times into generational cohorts (Dimock, 2019). For example, we align with Generation X because we were born between 1965 and 1980 (U.S. Bureau of Labor Statistics, 2022). Millennials were the next generation and consist of anyone born between 1981 and 1996. Anyone born between 1996 approximately 2012 belongs to a new generation called Generation Z, or GenZ (Dimock, 2019), which encompasses students entering college and the work force now.

GenZ students differ from other generations in that they grew up with cell phones, social media, and the internet. Over 93% of this generation engages in YouTube on a regular basis, and 71% watch more than three hours of online video per day (Huss, 2023). Knowledge is literally at their fingertips, and they are used to searching and locating answers on the internet, and more recently, using Artificial Intelligence. Faculty benefit from an understanding of what makes this generation unique. For example, it may be beneficial to recognize that these students often lack skills needed to discern the credibility of information. They may need assistance from professors, like Dr. Santos, identifying valuable, versus non-valuable, information. GenZ students may prefer that information be presented in a visual format, so instruction using a TED talk may be better received than any book or text reading on the same topic (Huss, 2023).

Faculty like Dr. Santos, charged with educating students, should be on the cutting edge, incorporating fresh approaches to learning, teaching, and thinking. Just as students grow and mature throughout their academic journey, new faculty grow and mature throughout their professional journey. As we describe quality teaching, we start with the basics. We have found through listening to our students that many faculty (and adjuncts) need a reminder about the basics.

## THE BASICS

Our students need passionate professors and consistent classroom expectations. Whether you teach at a small university or a large university, they want, and deserve, responsive professors. Based on fifteen years of focus group conversations with college students throughout the country, Arnsparger and Drivalas (2016) reported that student perspectives on college teaching align with research on teaching effectiveness that supports the importance of learning environments and experiences. By asking students to describe experiences that helped them achieve their academic goals, they (2016) found that students sought engaging pedagogies, high expectations, challenges and support, and contextualized learning. In addition, students appreciated faculty who knew how to teach and who were up to date on technology and content knowledge. Passionate teachers were also a desire, and students were okay with a lot of work when supported. Students appreciated high expectations, especially when faculty members reached out to provide assistance. Students valued authentic learning, in which they applied course content.

The students interviewed in the focus groups had reasonable expectations. In this section, we provide a list of basic teaching responsibilities which include Content, Student Focus and Management, Consistency, Promoting Student Engagement, and Self-Evaluation of Teaching. We feel these responsibilities are basic principles for professors to achieve as they work with undergraduate and graduate students. Many of the following criteria reflect those required of us at our university.

### Content

Course content of both new and seasoned professors should be up-to-date in their discipline. Delivering up-to-date and evidence-based material of course content is an essential element of teaching effectiveness. In addition, course content should include real world applications for learning and for the workplace (Kuh and O'Donnell, 2013). In other words, we are preparing our students for the real world, not just a test.

As we consider the relationship between the college student and college teacher, it is important to acknowledge that while a student is expected to perform the tasks required by a teacher, who will award a grade for the tasks, the teacher is expected to provide effective instruction. Faculty performance relates directly to student achievement and outcomes, specifically, how well faculty prepare students to attain their individual goals and succeed in their life's work (Soliday and Lombardi, 2018). Student success is a priority, and educating students in a higher education setting should entail fresh approaches to learning, teaching and thinking. Therefore, effective teaching includes a consideration for intentional course design, in which the instructor plans ways to present course content in a way that promotes understanding.

What role does academic freedom play in course development? Historically, it was not unusual for universities to dismiss faculty whose views were not aligned with the interests of the institution (De Witte, 2023). The concept of academic freedom changed this threat, reflecting the principle that scholars, researchers, and educators can engage in teaching and scholarship without the fear of losing their job. Academic freedom has a complex history. In his letter from a Birmingham Jail, Martin Luther King Jr. wrote, "To a degree, academic freedom is a reality today because Socrates practiced civil disobedience" (King, 1963, para. 17). This quote references Socrates' defense of himself against accusations that he corrupted the youth of Athens. He was eventually made to drink hemlock, resulting in death, as a punishment for his crimes.

In the U.S., the American Association of University Professors (AAUP), founded by John Dewey and Arthur Lovejoy, has played a significant role in defining and supporting academic freedoms (De Witte, 2023, May 1). The AAUP published the 1915 Declaration of Principles on Academic Freedom and Academic Tenure, intended to protect the "academic freedom" of the teacher and the student. The original German term for academic freedom used two words to describe this concept. "Lehrfreiheit" described the freedom to teach what one desires to teach, and "Lernfreiheit" described the freedom to learn in an academic setting without outside interference.

According to the declaration, academic freedom "comprises three elements: freedom of inquiry and research; freedom of teaching within the university or college; and freedom of extramural utterance and action" (AAUP, 1915, p. 292). On a global scale, the United Nations Educational, Scientific, and Cultural Organization (UNESCO) seeks to protect academic freedom. In 1993, the General Conference of the United Nations Educational, Scientific and Cultural Organization (UNESCO) devised and adopted an international recommendation on the status of higher education teaching personnel. Launched in June 2001 with startup funds from UNESCO, the Network on Education and Academic Rights (NEAR) serves as a clearing-house for information regarding attacks on academic freedom worldwide (UNESCO, 2001).

While academia enjoys academic freedom, please note that academic freedom maintains adherence to the scholarly profession as long as it aligns with the norms and standards of that discipline. In other words, freedom does not mean *any* content can be disseminated in a classroom. For instance, American history coursework should reflect the appropriated content, not that of a physics or business class. Academic freedom ensures that colleges and universities are "safe havens" for inquiry, places where faculty members like Dr. Santos can design courses that challenge students to exchange ideas, even when they contrast with traditional theories. Dr. Santos is free to select his preferred course materials relevant to the subject matter and to deliver instruction using a variety of pedagogical approaches (AAUP). However, academic freedom has limits in that faculty members must act ethically and professionally, teaching content that is valid and in alignment with professional regulations.

## Student Focus and Management

Kuh and O'Donnell (2013) were the first to identify eight key elements which make high-impact practices (HIPs) effective. We will visit HIPs in the next section but emphasize here, in this section on student focus, that the HIP's list of the eight key elements includes "frequent, timely, and constructive feedback" (para. 1); yet the following student focus items align with many complaints we hear from students:

- Post office hours and maintain your availability for students.
- Prepare an appropriate syllabus that is posted on the Learning Management System (LMS) before the first meeting of the class.
- Clearly explain course requirements and follow them. Follow policies and the calendar as set forth in the syllabus.
- Make effective use of class time. Regularly meet with the class during the entire scheduled time unless there are extenuating circumstances.
- Submit assignment grades (with corrective feedback) in a timely manner. *It is never okay to save all of your grading until the end of the semester.*
- Be fair and equitable.
- Appy strict adherence to student accommodations.
- Create a positive classroom culture.
- Demonstrate an interest in student progress.
- Respond to emails and other inquiries in a timely manner.
- Stimulate student thinking and engagement.
- Regularly contact students who are struggling with attendance or class performance.

In addition to these essential guidelines, preparedness for class is essential. We are not talking about being prepared academically to convey information or to answer questions. We are referring to the need to plan and to come to class ready to teach—never do anything last minute (Gasman, 2021). Planning for teaching effectiveness will be addressed further in the next chapter.

## Consistency

Just as professors seek consistency in faculty evaluations and employers seek consistency from their employees, students seek consistency from course instructors. The syllabus is a key component in maintaining consistency. Consider the syllabus to be a contract. Do not make changes to the contract after the course has begun. In addition, maintain consistency and fairness in grading. If you use Graduate Assistants for grading, train them to ensure reliability across graders.

## Promoting Student Engagement

Good teachers are able to engage their students in the content so that they want to learn. In turn, learners interact with course material actively rather than passively and make connections to their own lives. Strong teachers present challenges that further engage students to think critically (Buller, 2010). A simple way to engage students is by providing opportunities for them to speak and interact in class. Knowing students' names, visiting with them both in and out of class time, and inviting them to your office hours reinforces positive relationships. In the Mentoring Moments exercise for this chapter, we will encourage you to plan a few ice breakers you could use at the start of each class (f2f and online) to promote positive classroom environments.

## Self Evaluation of Teaching

As college professors, we seek to continuously improve our teaching. One way to do this is through the self-evaluation of teaching. In order to understand whether or not our teaching approach is effective, it is important to monitor student progress. If students do not understand course content or perform poorly on an exam, self-evaluation may be helpful in order to adjust teaching to meet student needs. It is appropriate to adjust instructional delivery to try to vary approaches. In addition, at the end of the semester, it is good practice to use assessment results to modify coursework and improve teaching. In the next section, we share teaching and learning practices that benefit all students, including learners from groups historically underserved by higher education (AACU, 2024).

## HIGH-IMPACT PRACTICES

The Association for American Colleges and Universities (AACU) publication on high-impact educational practices, by George Kuh (2008), has influenced colleges across the country. Kuh used data from the National Survey of Student Engagement and defined certain undergraduate student experiences as high-impact practices (HIPs). These practices were determined to have the potential to transform learners in higher education, particularly underserved students, including first generation students and racially minoritized populations. Efforts to improve retention rates have led to nationwide implementation of HIPs.

Kuh (2008) defined HIPs as evidence-based practices that positively engage students and impact student success. In order for an experience to be a HIP, it had to provide meaningful interactions between students, a variety of faculty members, and experts in the profession. HIPs represent enriching experiences such as learning communities, service learning, undergraduate research, internships, and senior culminating experiences and are positively associated with student engagement, deep and integration learning, and personal and educational gains for all students. More specifically, eleven HIPs and their descriptions can be found at https://www.aacu.org/trending-topics/high-impact. These practices include: capstone courses and projects, collaborative assignments and projects, common intellectual experiences, diversity/global learning, eportfolios, first year seminars and experiences, internships, learning communities, service learning and community-based learning, undergraduate research, and writing-intensive courses. Campus-wide implementation of such practices is common; however, practices such as collaborative assignments and projects, eportfolios, research, and service- and community-based learning can be incorporated into our coursework. We address these practices further in Chapter 2.

## BEYOND THE BASICS

The art of teaching is important. Student learning is the priority of all institutions of higher education and is directly related to teaching effectiveness (Kezar & Maxey, 2016). Therefore, universities require faculty to provide evidence of quality classroom teaching (Bakken & Simpson, 2011). When considering evidence of teaching effectiveness, faculty need to be reflective and intentional in improving teaching based on student success as well as student evaluations.

Penn State's Schreyer Institute for Teaching Excellence (n.d.) describes an excellent teacher as someone who "contributes positively to the learning environment by providing exceptional energy, keen interest in students, and extraordinary strengths" (para. 2). Excellence is further defined with five roles that constitute teaching excellence: subject matter expertise, pedagogical expertise, excellent communicator, student-centered mentor, systematic and continual assessor of their teaching. Of these roles professors take on, what is pedagogy?

### Pedagogy

Pedagogy is the method behind the art of teaching. Effective teachers understand the *how* of teaching, or pedagogy. Pedagogical decisions involve considerations of how to organize concepts, how to provide experiences necessary for understanding, how to best sequence instruction for conceptual development, and how to alleviate common confusions within a discipline that can be avoided or mediated with teaching strategies. Pedagogical decisions also reflect beliefs about learning related to student engagement. Which teaching models best support the targeted content goals? Problem-based strategies? Modeling and explicit instruction? Lecture and discussion? How will time be allocated for whole groups, small groups, and individual instruction, practice, and creation? Teaching and learning are also context-dependent. In addition to typical contextual differences such as socioeconomic status, student backgrounds, subject area, or language differences, access to devices and internet bandwidth affects the context for teaching and learning.

When designing lessons, teachers first consider the content and its organization. This type of understanding is called Content Knowledge (CK). Strong content knowledge includes both an abundance of knowledge and deep understandings of disciplinary structures and syntax. It includes the *why*, or theoretical underpinnings of the discipline. Teachers also consider how best to organize the instruction and what approaches work best for student understanding. This type of teacher knowledge is called Pedagogical Knowledge (PK). Pedagogical knowledge reflects an abundant and deep understanding of teaching and the instructional strategies to facilitate learning content or processes. Without strong PK, the most learned experts in a field may be unable to make concepts and content clear and comprehensible to the novice learner. Shulman (1987) labeled the intersection of Content Knowledge (CK) and Pedagogical Knowledge (PK) as Pedagogical Content Knowledge (PCK). The PCK model represents specialized teacher knowledge that reflects a teacher's understanding of how to deliver content effectively. Teachers with PCK understand which content-specific concepts and sub-processes challenge the learner, and they use particular pedagogical strategies to mediate learning. PCK occurs when pedagogy strengthens a teacher's ability to teach content competently and often distinguishes an effective and engaging teacher.

## Technology Integration

The ubiquitous presence of technology necessitates that college professors find meaningful ways to integrate it into their instruction and to leverage digital tools as additional supports for teaching and learning. Just as CK and PK were initially considered as separate silos of knowledge, Technology Knowledge (TK) was initially considered a separate domain of knowledge and skills. Mishra and Koehler (2006) recognized TK as a new teacher knowledge. They extended Shulman's idea of Pedagogical Content Knowledge and included TK as another knowledge domain. TK includes the knowledge of using information technology productively in both personal and work lives, knowing when it supports or hinders the attainment of a goal, and the ability to continue to adapt to technological change.

## WHAT IS TEACHING EFFECTIVENESS?

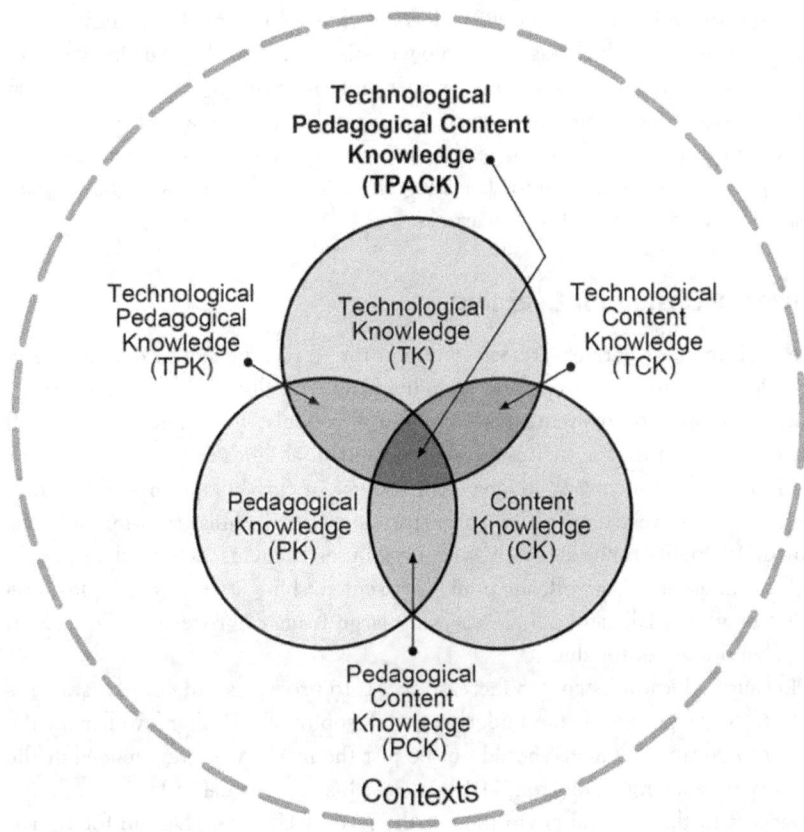

*Figure 1.1* The TPACK Model. Reproduced with permission of the publisher, © 2012 by tpack.org.

Because of this continuous change, there is no endpoint. Teachers will always be developing their TK. Including and integrating TK with PCK created a new framework for understanding the complexities of the knowledge domains teachers now need for 21st century teaching: Technological, Pedagogical and Content Knowledge (TPACK) (Figure 1.1).

TPACK creates additional knowledge intersections as well: Technological Content Knowledge (TCK), Technological Pedagogical Knowledge (TPK), and the complete integration of all three knowledge domains resulting in Technological, Pedagogical, and Content Knowledge, or TPACK (Mishra & Koehler, 2006). Understanding the intersections of these teacher knowledge domains affects successful technology integration (Koehler et al., 2013, p. 13). The point of sharing this model is to promote the consideration of technology integration in effective teaching. Technology integration can be as simple as using technology to accompany a lecture so that visual learners are accommodated. It can also be more complex, in which case technology tools transform the learning process. Online courses require intentional considerations for pedagogical practices. What practices work best in an online course? An abundance of research has been conducted on distance learning. Instead of presenting the research, we present the concept of Universal Design for Learning, in which the lessons (and courses) are designed for accessibility for all learners.

## Universal Design for Learning

The Architectural Barriers Act of 1968 and the Americans with Disabilities Act of 1990 prohibited the exclusion of individuals with disabilities from access to transportation, employment, public buildings, schools, goods and services, and other basic, everyday activities people without disabilities use. With access for *all* in mind, the concept of UD evolved. The use of curb cuts, ramps, escalators, elevators, large restroom stalls, automatic doors, and similar accommodations provided benefits for individuals with disabilities. Benefits extended to people without disabilities as well, including a parent pushing a stroller, people using crutches after a fall, and people carrying large loads of groceries who lack an extra hand to open the door.

Because educators strive to increase access to processes and content students need to learn in school, the underlying philosophy of UD aligns well with the goals of education, which "should not be just the mastery of knowledge but the mastery of learning" (Houston, 2018, p. 96). Just as the goal of UD is to design for access to the physical environment, the goal of Universal Design for Learning (UDL) is to design for access to the curricular goals and learning standards, enabling increased opportunities to reach all learners. Think about your students with hearing difficulties, vision issues, learning differences. UDL provides a framework for us to alleviate barriers to learning by considering (1) multiple means of engagement, (2) multiple means of representation, (3) multiple means of action and expression (CAST, 2024; Gordon, 2024; Meyer et al., 2014). See https://udlguidelines.cast.org/.

Accessibility in education is considered a basic human right (United Nations, 2016); therefore, the UDL framework is not limited to K-12 education. Since Universal Design for Learning operationalizes the right to education, it has the global attention of policymakers. International organizations like the International Society for Technology Education (ISTE) and the International Disability Alliance (IDA) champion UDL as a promising framework for inclusive instruction (ISTE, 2024; International Disability Alliance, 2021). In the U.S., the Higher Education Opportunity Act of 2008 federally defined and endorsed UDL.

UDL supports effective teaching through accessibility. Students taking online college courses may experience UDL principles in action (Pilgrim & Ward, 2017), as many universities incorporate standards like Quality Matters in online course development to ensure student access (Frey et al., 2012). Examples of tips for an accessible learning environment can be found at: https://www.qualitymatters.org/sites/default/files/pd-docs-PDFs/AccessibilityTipsHandout-NDLW-2017-webinar.pdf.

## SELF-MENTORSHIP

Let's now revisit Dr. Santos concerns as he begins his career in higher education. As faculty mentors, we suggest that Dr. Santos ask questions in the new faculty workshops. We would encourage him to take advantage of course team members, meaning other faculty who teach, or have taught, the same courses. Seeking help from colleagues builds relations and systems of support that could result in future collaboration. Apply chapter content to your own career and consider ways to engage GenZ students. Plan for ways to build a positive classroom environment, in person and virtually.

Through the practice of self-mentorship, you will develop your own personal and professional growth by seeking ways to build teaching effectiveness. In the Mentoring Moments section (Exercises 1.1-1.3), we provide an opportunity for you to develop icebreakers for f2f and online courses. You will investigate high-impact practices in higher education as well as technology integration to determine ways students can benefit from technology tools that provide a variety of support that enhances access to information.

## REFERENCES

AAUP (1915). 1915 Declaration of Principles on Academic Freedom and Academic Tenure. https://www.aaup.org/NR/rdonlyres/A6520A9D-0A9A-47B3-B550-C006B5B224E7/0/1915Declaration.pdf

Americans With Disabilities Act of 1990, 42 U.S.C. § 12101 et seq. (1990). https://www.ada.gov/pubs/adastatute08.htm

Arnsparger, A., & Drivalas, J. (2016). Students speak about faculty: What students need, what they want, and what helps them succeed. In A. Kezar & D. Maxey (Eds.), *Envisioning the faculty for the 21st century: Moving to a mission-oriented and learner-centered model* (pp. 101–116). Rutgers University Press.

The Association for American Colleges and Universities (2024). High impact practices. https://www.aacu.org/trending-topics/high-impact

Bakken, J. P., & Simpson, C. G. (2011). *A survival guide for new faculty members: Outlining the keys to success for promotion and tenure*. Charles C. Thomas.

Bain, K. (2004). *What the best college teachers do*. Harvard University Press.

Berardi, A. & Morton, B.M. (2019). *Trauma-Informed School Practices: Building expertise to transform schools*. Pennington Press.

Blaustein, M. E. (2013). Childhood trauma and a framework for intervention. In E. Rossen & R. Hull (Eds.), *Supporting and educating traumatized students: A guide for school-based professionals* (pp. 3–21). Oxford University.

Brint, S. (2018). *Two cheers for higher education: Why American universities are stronger than ever - and how to meet the challenges they face.* Princeton University Press.

Buller, J. L. (2010). *The essential college professor: A practical guide to an academic career.* Jossey-Bass.

Carrion, V. G., & Wong, S. S. (2012). Can traumatic stress alter the brain? Understanding the implications of early trauma on brain development and learning. *Journal of Adolescent Health, 51*(2), S23–S28.

Center for Applied Special Technology. (2018). Offer ways of customizing the display of information. Universal design for learning guidelines version 2.2. https://udlguidelines.cast.org/representation/perception/customize-display

Center for Applied Special Technology. (2024). Universal Design for Learning Guidelines version 3.0. https://udlguidelines.cast.org

Centers for Disease Control and Prevention. (2015). ACE study: major findings. Retrieved from http://www.cdc.gov/violenceprevention/acestudy/findings.html

Common Core State Standards Initiative. (2010). Common core state standards for English/language arts and literacy in history/social studies, science, and technical subjects. http://www.corestandards.org/

De Witte, M. (May 1, 2023). Academic freedom's origin story). *Stanford Report.* https://news.stanford.edu/stories/2023/05/origin-story-academic-freedom

Dimock, M. (2019). Defining generations: Where Millennials end and Generation Z begins. Pew Research Center. https://www.pewresearch.org/short-reads/2019/01/17/where-millennials-end-and-generation-z-begins/

Everly, G. S., & Lating, J. M. (2012). *A clinical guide to the treatment of the human stress response.* Springer.

Every Student Succeeds Act (2015). Pub. L. 114–95. Stat. 1177 (2015).

Felitti, V. J., Anda, R. F., Nordenberg, D., Williamson, D. F., Spitz, AlM., Edwards, V., Koss, M.P., & Marks, J.S. (1998). Relationship of childhood abuse and household dysfunction to many of the leading causes of death in adults: The adverse childhood experiences (ACE) study. *American Journal of Preventive Medicine, 14*(4), 245–258.

Fischer, K. (2022). The shrinking of higher ed. *The Chronicle of Higher Education.* https://www.chronicle.com/article/the-shrinking-of-higheer-ed

Fischman, W., & Gardner, H. (2022). *The real world of college: What higher education is and what it can be.* The MIT Press.

Flannery, M. E. (2023). The mental health crisis on college campuses. *NEA Today.* https://www.nea.org/nea-today/all-news-articles/mental-health-crisis-college-campuses

Frey, B. A., Kearns, L. R., & King, D. K. (2012). Quality Matters: Template for an accessibility policy for online courses. https://www.qualitymatters.org/sites/default/files/research-docs-pdfs/QM-Accessibility-Policy.pdf

Gasman, M. (2021). *Candid advice for new faculty members: A guide to getting tenure and advancing your academic career.* Myers Education Press.

Gordon, D. (Ed.) (2024). *Universal design for learning: Principles, framework, and practice.* CAST.

Hettiarachchy, J. (2021). A survival guide for college and university professors. Jay Hettiachchy.

The Higher Education Opportunity Act (2008). Pub. L. 110–315. *Stat. 3078* (2008). https://www.govinfo.gov/content/pkg/PLAW-110publ315/pdf/PLAW-110publ315.pdf

Houston, L. (2018). Efficient strategies for integrating universal design for learning in the online classroom. *Journal of Educators Online, 15*(3), 96–111, DOI: 10.9743/jeo.2018.15.3.4

Huss, J. A. (2023). Gen Z students are filling our online classrooms: Do our teaching methods need a reboot? *InSight: A Journal of Scholarly Teaching, 18*, 101–112.

International Disability Alliance. (2021). Universal Design for Learning and its role in ensuring access to inclusive education for all: A technical paper by the International Disability Alliance. https://www.internationaldisabilityalliance.org/sites/default/files/universal_design_for_learning_final_8.09.2021.pdf

International Society for Technology in Education. (2024). ISTE and CAST announce new partnership to elevate the EdTech landscape. https://iste.org/news/iste-and-cast-announce-new-partnership-to-elevate-the-edtech-landscape#:~:text=CAST%20will%20facilitate%20a%20training,insights%20into%20how%20humans%20learn

Kezar, A, & Maxey, D. (2016). *Envisioning the faculty for the twenty-first century: Moving to a mission-oriented and learner-centered model.* Rutgers University Press.

King, M. L. (April 16, 1963). Letter from a Birmingham Jail [King, Jr.] https://www.africa.upenn.edu/Articles_Gen/Letter_Birmingham.html

Koehler, M., Mishra, P., & Cain, W. (2013). What is technological pedagogical content knowledge? *Journal of Education, 193*(3). 13–18. https://www.jstor.org/stable/24636917

Kuh, G. D. (2008). High-impact educational practices: What they are, who has access to them, and why they matter. Association of American Colleges and Universities.

Kuh, G. D., & O'Donnell, K. (2013). *Ensuring quality & taking high-impact practices to scale.* American Association of Colleges and Universities.

Meyer, A., Rose, D. H., & Gordon, D. (2014). *Universal design for learning: Theory and practice.* CAST Professional Publishing.

Mishra, P., & Koehler, M. (2006). Technological pedagogical content knowledge: A framework for teacher knowledge. *Teachers College Record, 108*(6), 1017–1054. https://doi.org/10.1111/j.1467-9620.2006.00684.x

Morton, B. M. (2018). The grip of trauma: How trauma disrupts the academic aspirations of foster youth. *Child Abuse & Neglect. 74*, 73–81.

National Center for Education Statistics. (2022). Fall Enrollment component final data (2006–2021) and provisional data (2022). https://nces.ed.gov/ipeds/trendgenerator/app/answer/7/32#:~:text=In%20fall%202022%2C%20the%20full,is%20based%20on%205%2C706%20institutions

Perry, B. D. (2006). Fear and learning: Trauma-related factors in the adult education process. *New Directions for Adult and Continuing Education*, *2006*(110), 21–27.

Pilgrim, J, & Ward, A. K. (2017). Addressing diversity through the UDL lens. In E. Ortlieb, & E. Cheek (Eds.), *Addressing Diversity in Literacy Instruction. Literacy Research, Practice and Evaluation, Volume 8, 1–2* (pp. 231–252). Emerald Publishing Limited. ISSN: 2048–0458/doi:10.1108/S2048-045820170000008011

Schreyer Institute for Teaching Excellence (n.d.). Definition of teaching excellence. PennState. http://www.schreyerinstitute.psu.edu/Definition

Shulman, L. S. (1987). Knowledge and teaching: Foundations of the new reform. Harvard Educational Review, 57(1), 1–21

Soliday, J., & Lombardi, M. (2018). *Pivot.* Credo.

Souers, K., & Hall, P. (2016). *Fostering resilient learners: Strategies for creating a trauma-sensitive classroom*. Association of Supervision and Curriculum Development.

UNESCO. (2001). Politics and profit: Scholars at risk. *The Courier. UNESCO.* https://unesdoc.unesco.org/ark:/48223/pf0000124281

United Nations. (Sept. 1, 2016). Inclusive education vital for all, including persons with disabilities – UN rights experts. UN News: Global Perspective Human Stories. https://news.un.org/en/story/2016/09/537952#:~:text=Rather%2C%20the%20General%20Comment%20said,spaces%2C%20the%20General%20Comment%20stated

U.S. Bureau of Labor Statistics. (2022). Monthly labor review. https://www.bls.gov/opub/mlr/2022/article/time-use-of-millennials-and-generation-x-differences-across-time.htm

U.S. Congress. (1968). *Architectural Barriers Act of 1968*, Pub. L. No. 90-480, 82 Stat. 718. https://www.congress.gov/bill/90th-congress/house-bill/17419/text

van der Kolk, B. (2014). *The body keeps the score: Brain, mind, and body in the healing of trauma.* Penguin.

Vermetten, E., & Bremner, J. D. (2002). Circuits and systems in stress: Preclinical studies. *Depression and Anxiety*, *15*(3), 126–147. https://doi.org/10.1002/da.10016

Vostanis, P. (2017). Editorial: Global child mental health: Emerging challenges and opportunities. *Child and Adolescent Mental Health*, *22*, 177-178. https://doi.org/10.1111/camh.12246

Chapter 2

# Preparing for Teaching Effectiveness

## FACULTY FOCUS

Dr. Gonzales, a newly hired professor in the History Department, had always envisioned herself inspiring students to think critically about the past. After years of studying and publishing on historical narratives, she was eager to bring her passion into the classroom. She knew it would take work to plan and develop assignments that aligned with her philosophy of teaching. As the start of the semester approached, excitement gave way to anxiety as she realized how much work lay ahead. Her teaching load was heavy: two face-to-face (f2f) classes and one fully online course. Each course required a comprehensive syllabus, engaging assignments, and a functional setup in the university's Learning Management System (LMS). The LMS was completely unfamiliar to her, and while she had watched a tutorial during orientation, the platform felt more like a labyrinth than a helpful tool. Meanwhile, her inbox buzzed constantly with reminders and new tasks. The department chair sent a message about syllabus guidelines. Disability and Testing Services forwarded a list of students requiring accommodations, with instructions on how to apply them in the LMS. The library asked for textbook submissions, and students from her online course had already emailed questions about access to materials. Each task seemed urgent and essential. Dr. Gonzales wanted her courses to be engaging and accessible, but the weight of looming deadlines made it hard to focus. It was hard to not feel like she was falling behind before the semester had even begun.

## INTRODUCTION

Strategic preparation helps guide the teaching process and aligns it with curriculum and program goals, setting the stage for an effective learning experience in which both the teacher and the students know what is expected to be achieved. It may also alleviate some of the stress Dr. Gonzales is experiencing. This chapter helps new faculty understand the importance of effectively implementing your philosophy of teaching. Our goal is to share ways to plan for teaching effectiveness, including the consideration of course outcomes and assessment and the development of an effective course syllabus.

## IMPLEMENTING YOUR TEACHING PHILOSOPHY

If you are currently a new faculty member, you probably shared your teaching philosophy when you applied for your faculty position. If you did not, you will likely be asked for a teaching statement at some point during your career. Your teaching philosophy serves as a foundation for intentional and reflective teaching practices that lead to meaningful educational experiences for students. It is for this reason that it is often required or a recommended part of a tenure portfolio. Since a statement of teaching philosophy reflects your core beliefs about teaching and learning (Chism, 1997–1998), it includes your definition of good teaching, your explanation of the teaching methods you use to engage students in your content, an overview of your assessment methods, and a reflection on professional growth, including ways you continually improve your teaching (Chism, 1997–1998).

A teaching philosophy requires self-reflection and serves as a foundation for syllabus development. In planning for teaching effectiveness, one must determine how to best implement one's teaching philosophy or the learning theory with which one best aligns. Learning theories help us understand how students acquire knowledge and how learning occurs. For example, John Dewey (1938) promoted the benefits of experiential learning, explaining, "there is an intimate and necessary relation between the processes of experience and education" (p. 7). He asserted that experiential learning enables students to develop their own opinions of a concept based on interaction with information. A professor who values constructivism (Vygotsky, 1978) and experiential learning (Dewey, 1938) may include hands-on, collaborative projects in their coursework.

In educational frameworks, this intentional focus on instructional delivery is referred to as "pedagogy," which we addressed in Chapter 1 as the art and science of teaching. However, the term *andragogy* is often preferred in higher education (Smith, 2002). This preference is a result of the differences between educating children and educating adults. The term *pedagogy* includes the Greek root *peda*, which means *child*, and the term *andragogy* includes the Greek root *andra*, which means *adult* (Smith, 2002). In contrast to a pedagogical stance on learning, Malcolm Knowles (1970) promoted *andragogy* because he believed adults learn differently from children. Knowles' theory on adult learning was grounded in his belief that adult learning had to be self-driven. He believed adults need to be involved in planning and evaluating their work and that adults are most interested in content that is relevant and applicable (Knowles, 1984). Below, we share our teaching philosophy statements along with an explanation of how the statements impacted syllabus development.

## Jodi's Teaching Philosophy

As a literacy educator, I equip preservice teachers with the skills to implement effective and inclusive literacy instruction. It is my responsibility to shape not only the minds of my preservice teachers but also the educational experiences of the future students they will serve. My teaching philosophy is grounded in the belief that learning occurs through experiences in which students learn by doing (Dewey, 1938). Experiential learning aligns with a constructivist approach in which students learn by doing. Therefore, experiential learning includes fieldwork and classroom applications. Instead of telling my students how to teach, I *show* them and provide them with opportunities to practice in authentic classroom environments. My goal is to equip aspiring educators with the knowledge and skills necessary for effective teaching.

My teaching strategies include evidence-based practices, which students learn and then apply to their field experiences. After watching my students teach, I provide immediate and corrective feedback. Therefore, performance assessments are designed to align with course objectives and to provide data on the progression of teaching skills. To foster motivation, I connect course content to the real-world challenges and opportunities educators face. To ensure students are equipped with tools for a rapidly evolving educational landscape, I promote technology integration and multiliteracies, focusing on skills required for success in the 21st century.

My teaching philosophy extends to my online classes, in which my physical presence is lacking. In order to facilitate an active learning community, I build connections through consistent and clear communication. I implement pedagogical approaches that use technology tools to facilitate active participation in an environment where students feel connected and supported in their learning. In addition, I emphasize the importance of critical thinking in learning. Although critical thinking is a goal for all students to apply and use as they build their knowledge and skills, it is especially important in online coursework. In a digital world, students across all disciplines need to be able to evaluate and discern authentic information from "fake" information. Fake news threatens information access, which is a basic right of all citizens (Loos, et al., 2018). Therefore, to be efficient consumers of information, students must apply critical thinking, which Dewey (1933) considered to be a stance or disposition in which a learner actively applies reflective thought. I believe opportunities for critical thinking should be a part of learning environments.

## *Application to Syllabi*

One of the literacy courses I teach is a field-based course. Half of the course is f2f instruction on campus. The other half of the course takes place at a local elementary school for my elementary teacher candidates and at a middle school for my middle school teacher candidates. Students are assigned to a classroom at the beginning of the semester. Throughout the course of the semester, students learn about the components of an effective reading program (phonological awareness, phonics, vocabulary, fluency, and comprehension). Then, students use their knowledge and new skills to teach lessons in their field assignments. Students in this course gain hands-on experiences, which, as outlined in my philosophy of teaching, provide them with authentic opportunities to practice teaching skills. Course objectives, course assignments, and course assessments align with this perspective. When developing the course syllabus, I make sure to include explicit instructions for lesson development. A rubric is provided so students understand the expectations for the lesson. Before students teach, I evaluate and provide feedback on their work in case changes need to be made before lesson implementation. When ready, students teach the lesson to their assigned classroom (or small group). A rubric is also used as I evaluate lesson delivery. This is just one component of the course outcomes and assessments, but the alignment to my teaching philosophy is evident. The course exams are also application-based so that students must analyze case study scenarios and apply authentic teaching skills.

Field-based courses align well with experiential learning. It was a bit more of a challenge to design my online course for secondary teachers, who need to understand disciplinary literacy. I was intentional about applying my philosophy of teaching to the course assignments. Engaging students in online courses is difficult—at times it takes more work than f2f courses. The assignments I embedded are teaching strategies I would like my students to use in their own classroom to support literacy skills. Therefore, textbook reading assignments each week required students to explore reading strategies and to discuss them with their peers. I planned for students to engage in content literacy activities, which they would one day model for their own students. My course included anticipation guides, double entry journals, and other reading strategies. I supported our online learning community by offering weekly virtual meetings, where students could come to ask questions or go over the provided lesson. We engaged in discussions once a week, and I was intentional on designing application-based assignments (teaching strategies) that would not seem like busy work to students. For example, one week, students were assigned parts of a chapter to summarize using audio QR codes (vocaroo.com), which they could use in the future with Emerging Bilinguals in their classroom. Another discussion board required students to share websites they found with games they could use for vocabulary development. The course final exam required students to apply the strategies they learned – they read a case study and wrote a response in which they applied the knowledge and skills they gained about teaching.

The teaching statement mentioned multiliteracies. While traditional alphabetic literacies are important, multiple ways of communicating have shifted the boundaries of literacy to include multiliteracies, which involve visual and audio modes of communication represented through print, audio, video, or graphics (Kress, 2003; New London Group, 1996). In my online course, I allow students to use multiple modes of communication in many assignments.

## Brenda's Teaching Philosophy

In 2011, I had the privilege of sitting with foster youth and listening to their stories. Each story was filled with hurt, trauma, and hope. One by one, each foster youth shared the role of a teacher in their lives. I learned that they all had at least one teacher during their academic career that they knew cared about them, held them to a high standard, and supported them every step of the way. This confirmed for me that as teachers, we have an awesome responsibility and opportunity to speak into the lives of our students. But, to do so, we must plan well to create a classroom environment that welcomes all students, assess our students in meaningful ways, and engage as lifelong learners.

My philosophy of teaching has been informed by several individuals. They include John Dewey and Lev Vygotsky, who explained the power of active learning, which includes involving students in the curriculum, and creating opportunities for exploration and interaction with their environment. Their theories can be seen in my classrooms through short lectures followed by practice, group activities, and hands-on learning. This includes case studies, role play, and real-world challenges. I learned about the significance of attachment theory, and how it influences the learning process and neurobiological development, from Dr. Perry (2009) and Dr. van der Kolk (2014). They explained specifically how trauma impairs the brain, influences interactions with others, and causes health challenges throughout the lifespan. Their work has transformed the way I mentor and train educational leaders. Understanding that students may not be in control of their behaviors requires a shift in how educators address classroom management. From Dr. Kinniburgh and Dr. Blaustein (2005), I learned how to create a strong foundation for learning through their attachment, regulation, and competency model. This supports all learners, but in particular those who have had a traumatic past. In my classes, I emphasize and model what it means to provide a safe learning environment that fosters attachment. My course creation, activities, classroom culture, assessment, and commitment to lifelong learning all tie back to these theorists and experts.

Creating a strong class requires time and intentionality. It requires a classroom environment where students feel safe, seen, and welcome. It must include thoughtful assessments that provide accurate measures of learning. It also requires an educator dedicated to their craft and committed to lifelong learning so as to keep their own classes and practices current. I carefully construct each class session to maximize learning and engagement. My courses require active student participation and engagement. I employ multiple teaching strategies and practices, which include class discussions, case studies, role- play, group presentations, and individual reflections. I also use technology to enhance our learning and to model what they could do in their own P-16 schools.

Having learned that more than 60% of students have been impacted by trauma, I now approach my classes a bit differently. I realize that before students can learn, they need to feel safe, seen, and welcomed. If I do not keep this as my first priority, I will not be able to reach all students. When students feel safe, they will allow themselves to be transparent and vulnerable. I have found this leads to the best learning for the student and their classmates. To create this kind of an environment, I believe I too must be vulnerable and transparent. By sharing my own story of failures and accomplishments and by showing respect for my students, I have found I am able to get to know my students on a deeper level, which allows for the largest growth. I also believe in creating critical thinkers and problem solvers. My students know that we construct our knowledge together by wrestling with difficult topics through a lens of content, social justice, and grace. Therefore, I create space for students to bring challenges from their P-16 schools into our class so that students can discuss and identify solutions together. I contribute to the learning but I am not the sole source of knowledge.

Assessing knowledge and skill attainment is essential. Therefore, I create assessments for my classes that include multiple opportunities for students to demonstrate their learning. Each assessment includes clear instructions and rubrics. I encourage my students to consider a solution or idea from multiple perspectives and then re-analyze their solution from a different point of view. This expands their thinking and understanding of the needs of diverse learners in their classrooms.

As an educator and lifelong learner I believe it is my responsibility to stay current on educational topics. To accomplish this, I read books and conduct research. I believe these activities, along with my scholarship, allow me to create classes with relevant content that prepare my students to become strong educational leaders.

### *Application to Syllabi*

One of the courses I teach is a research class with doctoral students. This course is a hybrid model with five f2f class sessions and four robust modules between each f2f class. As I mentioned in my philosophy of teaching, I create opportunities for student exploration and interaction with their environment. In this particular research class, we take a deep dive into qualitative methodology. One assignment the students enjoy includes students working in pairs, creating one or several research question(s), drafting interview questions, conducting the interviews, and then bringing their data to class. Students take turns sharing their experience and walking through challenges they encountered and their reflection on the experience. I model one way to analyze qualitative data. Students take what they learned and apply it to the data they collected. They then share their findings with their peers, engage in conversation about the decisions they made along the way, and ask for feedback. Knowledge is constructed together, leveraging student strengths and backgrounds.

Another course I teach is on trauma and how we can use knowledge of the impact of trauma to advocate for others in our community. This is an online course, which can make it a bit tricky due to the sensitive nature of the content. I plan all my courses with intentionality, but for this one in particular I must consider how the readings, discussions, activities, and assignments could be difficult for some people. While I know the majority of students in any of my classes may have been impacted by trauma, I have found that I tend to have more than the statistical average in this course. Therefore, I begin this course by clearly outlining the assignments and including rubrics so that students are able to find the expectations. I also am careful to point out material that could be difficult for some so that they are not caught by surprise. I set expectations how students should share and what to consider before responding to their classmate's online posts. I talk about honoring all voices and how we create and maintain a safe space. And I differentiate my instruction to meet the needs of students who may need some additional support or material due to their own history of trauma. By the end of the semester, I am proud of the community we have created and their desire to support others.

## PLANNING

We share our philosophies and how we apply our core values to our classroom instruction in order to demonstrate how effective teaching requires careful and intentional planning. We work hard to ensure that our instructional strategies, learning activities, and assessments align with our educational goals. Dr. Gonzales began planning early, which is key to a successful semester. Early and collaborative planning enables her to identify systems of support offered by the university. As a new faculty member, she will want to find out how syllabi are developed in her department and proceed in syllabus development based on the information she obtains. Typically, every department maintains a copy of each syllabus used throughout the semesters for their records. She should have access to at least one syllabus to use as a guide in preparing her course syllabus.

Ideally, universities would have support systems in place as new faculty begin planning their course curricula. We mentioned in the previous chapter that many universities provide support through centers for teaching and learning. In addition, Dr. Gonzales should seek the support of her co-workers in the history department, especially those who teach different sections of the same course. Bakken (2011) calls these "instructional course teams" (p. 71). Collaborating with instructional course teams benefits both students and faculty. Students gain similar experiences regardless of the professor, which helps with program consistency. Instructors gain support through a co-planning experience in which instructors of the same course have an opportunity to discuss topics like course content, course standards, course schedule, course texts or materials, assessments, course projects, and grading standards (Bakken, 2011), which is especially useful to new faculty. These are all topics that are included in the course syllabi. Dr. Gonzales may have questions about expectations related to the content she is passionate about.

## THE BASICS
### The Syllabus

Educators use the Latin word *syllabus,* meaning "list," for the outline of course objectives and course activities (vocabulary.com, 2024). A syllabus is far more than a list, though. The syllabus is a required document, which outlines what students agree to complete in order to achieve objectives and demonstrate learning in your course (The University of Texas, 2024). Consider it to be a contract between you and your students (Parkes and Harris, 2002). In the case of a grade appeal, faculty members will either win or lose an appeal based on their observance of the evaluation system indicated on the syllabus. Most universities require the syllabus to be provided on or before the first day of class. In addition, after it has been posted, the expectations should not be changed.

Many universities opt to include university-wide syllabus templates, which include policy statements that reflect rules and guidelines all faculty and students must follow. A standard syllabus provides consistency for accreditation purposes. In our standard template (Simple Syllabus), our course descriptions are generated for us. This ensures faculty members do not change the course description. The course description was determined and written by the program and approved by a curriculum committee. It cannot be revised at the whim of a new faculty member. Other standard features of a syllabus may include policies related to grade appeals, academic integrity, drops and withdrawals, and disability and accommodation statements reflecting university policies. At our university, those statements are provided for us in our template and are non-negotiable. Other primary syllabus features include contact information, course information, course objectives, program-learning outcomes, course delivery and credit hours, textbooks and materials, and assignments and grading policies. In addition, the syllabus should include a calendar of assignments due dates. These syllabus components are described and discussed in more detail in the next section.

### Instructor Information

As instructors supporting student learnings, it is important we provide details for our students' success, including your name, contact information (email, phone, office location), and office hours. Office hours, which provide an opportunity for students to seek help, are important to maintain. During COVID, online meeting links became a way for students to meet with their instructors. This trend has continued, and many professors include a Zoom or Teams personal meeting link to meet with students virtually.

## Course Information

Syllabi include the course title, code, semester, location, and meeting times. Students should be able to easily determine when and where the course takes place. In addition, a course description is an important feature that provides a brief summary of what the course will cover.

### Learning Objectives

Outcomes-based teaching and learning (Spady, 1994) is an educational approach that focuses on what students learn rather than what they are taught. This concept targets student learning by explicitly defining the desired learning outcomes at the beginning of a course or program, then designing teaching and assessment activities to ensure students achieve the specific goals, putting the emphasis on what students will be able to do rather than just what the instructor is teaching (Spady, 1994; Rao, 2020). A learning outcome is a description of what students will learn and how that learning will be assessed. Therefore, a syllabus should include clearly defined outcomes stated in measurable terms. Spending time developing course learning outcomes (CLOs) benefits the instructor by providing a framework for the course content and sequence, communicating to students what they must do, and conveying transparency related to assessment of learning (Stanford, n.d.). Student benefits are similar, since learners can use the outcomes to concentrate on areas they need to develop in the course.

Some accrediting bodies may require program learning objectives or learning outcomes be included on a syllabus as well. Program learning objectives (PLOs) reflect knowledge and skills students should be able to demonstrate after completion of an entire program. For example, my course objective may be that my teacher candidates learn phonics terminology and generalizations. The learning outcome is that they can teach first graders how to read using phonics instruction. Where CLOs align with course assessment, PLOs align with program assessment. CLOs are crucial in planning for teaching effectiveness. They offer a clear, measurable framework for designing targeted teaching methods, select relevant content, and develop appropriate assessments to ensure students achieve the desired learning goals.

### Course Delivery and Credit Hours

Course delivery tells students if a course will be online, in the classroom, in the field, or hybrid (a mixture of all three). Factors that determine course delivery include the timing and location of the course environment. Two terms worth considering are synchronous and asynchronous learning. Synchronous learning occurs in real-time, at a designated time and space, like a campus classroom or a virtual space, using platforms like Zoom or Teams (Stanford, n.d.). Asynchronous learning provides students with the opportunity to access course materials and resources at any time from any location (Stanford, n.d.). Traditional learning is typically f2f learning in a classroom. Online courses occur within a Learning Management System, like Canvas or Blackboard.

Most traditional courses consist of three credit hours, which represents a set amount of time students spend studying with a teacher. The federal definition of a credit hour is:

> (1) One hour of classroom or direct faculty instruction and a minimum of two hours of out of class student work each week for approximately fifteen weeks for one semester or trimester hour of credit, or ten to twelve weeks for one quarter hour of credit, or the equivalent amount of work over a different amount of time; or (2) At least an equivalent amount of work as required in paragraph (1) of this definition for other academic activities as established by the institution including laboratory work, internships, practica, studio work, and other academic work leading to the award of credit hours. (SACSCOC, 2023, para. 4–5)

The history of the credit hour is worth mentioning in an age of declining student enrollment and concern for student retention. The credit hour was established by the Carnegie Foundation for the Advancement of Teaching (n.d.) and is often referred to as the Carnegie unit. The Carnegie unit is sometimes criticized on the basis that we are measuring time rather than learning. Programs advocating mastery of content rather than time-based units include Competency-Based Education programs (CBEs).

## Resources

### People

Depending on the nature of the course you teach, there may be a need to include resources for students to use for additional help. As an undergraduate literacy professor, I include our library liaison as a resource for my students. An English class may include the university's writing center personnel. A doctoral syllabus might include resources like the research center staff.

### Textbooks and Materials

The use of textbooks combined with lecture and discussion supports all students by offering multiple learning sources that cater to diverse learning styles and reinforce for active engagement with course content. I had a student ask me in class one time why they had to have a textbook if we were going to cover everything in class. First of all, there is certainly no way to cover everything in a textbook in class. This particular student was academically gifted and was able to grasp course material easily. I explained to her that not only does the textbook and other readings serve as a way to build depth of knowledge, but it could also be a preferred way of learning content for some students. Some students are visual learners and learn through class discussions while others need time to explore the content on their own. Course materials like textbooks and other readings (articles, videos, and more) support the knowledge base of our course content. The content covered in class should be evidence-based, and contain content accepted in the field of study. Therefore, even if we do not require our students to buy a textbook, we should include materials in our syllabus that support the material covered over the course of a semester. It is important for faculty to spend time reviewing textbooks in their discipline, seeking the most updated and accessible materials for our students. Consider the textbook costs your students will be asked to endure as you search for course-related materials.

## Open Access Materials

A trend gaining momentum in education is the use of Open Access (OA) materials, defined as "digital, online, free of charge, and free of most copyright and licensing restrictions," (Suber, 2015, para. 1). With the support of their administration, many college professors have been replacing expensive commercial textbooks with no-cost Open Educational Resources (OER) to help make college more affordable for their students (Griswold, 2022). OER publishing has increased in general (Blankstein, 2023), but locating free materials may be difficult depending on your discipline. If you are interested in finding free materials for students to use in your classroom, you might check with your university's librarian. You could also examine materials via the Creative Commons Search Portal (https://resources.creativecommons.org/).

## Policies

We briefly mentioned university policies included in course syllabi. In addition, our Faculty Focus also mentioned that Dr. Gonzales had questions about student accommodations, which is understandable. The Americans with Disabilities Act (ADA) (1990) and Section 504 of the Rehabilitation Act (1973) mandate that all institutions receiving federal funding must provide reasonable accommodations to students with disabilities. The purpose of these laws is to ensure equal access for people with disabilities and to protect them against discrimination. Therefore, if a student provides evidence they need a specific accommodation, such as extra time on exams, they may be eligible to receive it in college. Federal law requires you follow the accommodation information carefully.

## Grading Policies

Grading policies can be university-wide policies. For example, when I (Jodi) started as a new faculty member at UMHB, the university-wide grading scale was set. A student had to earn a 91 or above for an A, an 81 or above for a B, and so on. Colleges or departments may have grading policies as well. For example, attendance (or lack thereof) can often impact a course grade. Check with colleagues regarding the policies already in place. Late work can also impact grades. We offer the same advice in the case of late work. If you have the flexibility to set your own policy, it is important to be consistent.

## Calendar

A course calendar provides information about topics, activities, and assignment due dates. Many professors mark their calendars as tentative to allow for minor changes in the scope and sequence of course content. A tentative course calendar accommodates unexpected events or issues as well as adaptability to current events and flexibility with content topics that need extra instruction.

## BEYOND THE BASICS: PLANNING FOR CLASS

The content of a syllabus sets the tone for the entire semester and requires considerable planning for the implementation of course content, including the delivery of lessons throughout a semester. Wiggins and McTighe's (2011) Understanding by Design framework is an excellent resource in understanding this complexity. They promote three stages of "backward design," in which instructors first identify desired results (CLOs), then create assessments which will allow us to determine how we will know if students have achieved the desired results? Determining this information based on evidence is discussed in Chapter 3. The last component of backward design is planning learning experiences and instruction. Instructors plan the most appropriate lessons and learning activities in order for students to attain the learning outcomes. Learning activities should be considered prior to the start of the semester and outlined in the syllabus.

Online courses require a different kind of planning. Engaging students in an online environment is a challenge. A part of the challenge will involve becoming familiar with the online platform, or Learning Management System (LMS), used by your university. Our university uses Canvas, which is user-friendly. However, expect a learning curve as you gain experience navigating online tools, including video conferencing tools as well as tools that promote interaction in online environments. If used effectively, LMS will provide supports for students unimaginable 10 years ago.

## Learning Management Systems (LMS)

Dr. Gonzales needs to set up her LMS, which should be aesthetically pleasing and user-friendly for students. As she is new to the university, it may be helpful for her to see examples of well-organized classes in her university's LMS system. To do so, she could ask her department chair for recommendations of faculty for her to connect with, or ask colleagues if they are willing to share information on how they organize their courses. We would also recommend that Dr. Gonzales solicit feedback from her students early in the semester on their experience thus far with her class setup in the LMS.

## Content Delivery

Preparing for each class, especially the first time a class is taught, is time-consuming. Some of the simpler tasks would be to make sure she is familiar with the technology in her classrooms. Dr. Gonzales must determine the best way to design learning activities in both her online and f2f courses, considering discussions and group work. She might prefer to use the Socratic method, which uses open-ended questions to help students develop critical thinking skills and a deeper understanding of a topic. She must determine the materials she will use for her lesson—slides, videos, discussion. She must apply management skills to build community, encourage participation, and handle sensitive topics.

## Accommodations

Our Faculty Focus highlighted Dr. Gonzales' anxiety related to early semester information overload, including the receipt of student accommodations. Unless education is your background or you have children who receive accommodations, you may be unfamiliar with what this means at a university level. The Americans with Disabilities Act (ADA) (1990) mandates that postsecondary institutions provide necessary accommodations when a student discloses a disability. Faculty members must ensure that students have access to the accommodations for which they are approved. What does this mean? Basically, compliance with this law is required. You need to read accommodations carefully, call disability services with any questions you have, and ensure the information remains confidential. Accommodation categories typically ensure the following:

- Presentation accommodations require instruction or assessment in an alternate format. Some examples include ASL, captioning, assistive technology devices, Braille, large print, or a reader.

- Response accommodations allow students to complete assignments or exams in different ways (e.g., use of reference aids, clicker, use of computer, etc.).
- Timing/Scheduling accommodations increase the allowable length of time to complete a test or assignment and may also change the way the time is organized (e.g., extended time, frequent breaks).
- Setting accommodations change the location in which a test or assignment is given or the conditions of the assessment setting (e.g., private exam room, distraction-reduced). (UCLA, 2025., para. 5)

## SELF-MENTORSHIP

Do you become overwhelmed easily? Do you flounder under deadlines? Self-mentorship involves identifying your strengths and weaknesses, so self-awareness of your potential stressors is important as you plan for teaching effectiveness. Setting goals and seeking additional learning opportunities will enable you to prepare for your academic semester. Think back to the new tasks Dr. Gonzales faced at the beginning of the year and consider ways you can plan ahead for these situations. As faculty mentors, we would encourage Dr. Gonzales to use resources available, including her peers and materials from previously taught sections of her courses, as she plans for her semester. Developing syllabi and delivering lessons can be overwhelming with new preps. Planning gets easier the more times a professor has taught a class.

Apply your own philosophies of learning to your future career as you develop your own professional growth towards teaching effectiveness. What essential elements will you include in the syllabus? What instructional approaches will you use? How will you organize the LMS? The Mentoring Moments exercises (Exercises 2.1-2.3) will prompt you to think about and develop a written teaching philosophy. In addition, the exercises support your professional learning as you practice writing learning outcomes. Finally, you will research appropriate textbooks and resources that align with your subject matter, examining materials for quality and cost.

## REFERENCES

Americans with Disabilities Act of 1990, 42 U.S.C. § 12101 (1990).

Bakken, J. P., & Simpson, C. G. (2011). A survival guide for new faculty members: Outlining the keys to success for promotion and tenure. Charles C. Thomas.

Blankstein, M. (2023, Jan. 11). The library's role with open educational resources: A conversation with librarians. ITHAKA S+R. https://sr.ithaka.org/blog/the-librarys-role-with-open-educational-resources/

Carnegie Foundation for the Advancement of Teaching. (n.d.). The Carnegie unit. https://www.carnegiefoundation.org/about/faqs/the-carnegie-unit/

Chism, N. V. N. (1997–98). Developing a philosophy of teaching statement. *Essays on teaching excellence: Toward the best in the academy, 9*(3). http://podnetwork.org/content/uploads/V9-N3-Chism.pdf

Dewey, J. (1933). *How we think: A restatement of the relation of reflective thinking to the educative process.* D.C. Heath & Co Publishers. https://bef632.wordpress.com/wp-content/uploads/2015/09/dewey-how-we-think.pdf

Dewey, J. (1938). *Experience in education.* New York: MacMillan.

Griswold, R. H. (2022). Access is not enough: An examination of OER textbook usage by English composition students at one community college. *Community College Enterprise, 28*(6), 62–76. https://research-ebsco-com.dewey.umhb.edu/linkprocessor/plink?id=fd5c2f0b-0245-3f2b-9958-47f6eeb080f3 Acesso em: 11 nov. 2024.

Kinniburgh, K. J., Blaustein, M., Spinazzola, J., & Van Der Kolk, B. A. (2005). Attachment, self-regulation, and competency. *Psychiatric Annals, 35*(5), 424–430.

Knowles, M. S. (1970). *The modern practice of adult education: Andragogy verus pedagogy.* Association Press.

Knowles, M. S. (1984). *Andragogy in action.* Jossey-Bass.

Kress, G. (2003). *Literacy in the new media age.* Routledge.

Loos, E., Ivan, L., Leu, D. (2018). Save the pacific northwest tree octopus: A hoax revisited. Or: How vulnerable are school children to fake news? *Information and Learning Science*, 2018. https://doi.org/10.1108/ILS-04-2018-0031

New London Group. (1996). A pedagogy of multiliteracies: Designing social futures. *Harvard Educational Review, 66*(1), 60–92. https://doi.org/10.17763/haer.66.1.17370n67v22j160u

Parkes, J., & Harris, M. B. (2002). The purposes of a syllabus. *College Teaching, 50*(2), 55–61.

Perry, B. D. (2009). Examining child maltreatment through a neurodevelopmental lens: Clinical applications of the neurosequential model of therapeutics. *Journal of Loss and Trauma, 14*(4), 240–255.

Rao, N. J. (2020). Outcome-based Education: An Outline. *Higher Education for the Future, 7*(1), 5–21. https://doi.org/10.1177/2347631119886418

Section 504 of the Rehabilitation Act of 1973 (29 U.S.C." Code of Federal Regulations, title 28 (2002):516–544. https://www.govinfo.gov/app/details/CFR-2002-title28-vol1/CFR-2002-title28-vol1-sec35-104

Smith, M. K. (2002). Malcolm Knowles, informal adult education, self-direction and andragogy. *The Encyclopedia of Pedagogy and Informal Education.* https://infed.org/mobi/malcolm-knowles-informal-adult-education-self-direction-and-andragogy/

Southern Association of Colleges and Schools. (2023). Credit hours. https://sacscoc.org/app/uploads/2019/08/Credit-Hours.pdf

Spady W. G. (1994). *Outcome-based education: Critical issues and answers.* Arlington, VA: American Association of School Administrators.

Stanford University (n.d.). Course planning. https://teachingcommons.stanford.edu/teaching-guides/foundations-course-design/course-planning

Suber, P. (2015). Open access overview. http://bit.ly/oa-overview

The University of Texas. (2024). Your syllabus at UT Austin. The University of Texas Office of the Executive Vice President and Provost. https://provost.utexas.edu/the-office/academic-affairs/your-syllabus-at-ut-austin/

UCLA. (2025). Accommodations 101. Center for Accessible Education. https://cae.ucla.edu/faculty-handbook/accommodation-101

van Der Kolk, B. (2014). *The body keeps the score: Brain, mind, and body in the healing of trauma.* New York, NY: Penguin.

Vocabulary.com (2024). Syllabus. https://www.vocabulary.com/dictionary/syllabus#:~:text=The%20noun%20syllabus%20comes%20from,That's%20the%20syllabus.

Vygotsky, L. (1978). Interaction between learning and development. In M. Cole, V. John-Steiner, S. Scribner, & E. Souberman (Eds.), *Mind in society: The development of higher psychological process* (pp. 79–91). Harvard University Press.

Wiggins, G., & McTighe, J. (2011). *The Understanding by Design guide to creating high-quality units.* ASCD.

Chapter 3

# Evaluating Teaching Effectiveness

## FACULTY FOCUS

*Dr. Potter is a new undergraduate faculty member in the Math department, who has just reviewed his students' evaluations of teaching (SET). Dr. Potter is discouraged. After pouring many hours into planning for teaching effectiveness and working hard to provide student feedback, Dr Potter has received low SET scores. Few students left constructive comments, so he does not know why the students were so critical. He maintained consistent office hours and encouraged students to visit him for help. He feels confident that he developed fair quiz and exam questions. Understanding that student SET could impact his faculty evaluation, Dr. Potter wonders what steps he should take next to demonstrate his efforts to provide effective instruction and supportive practices.*

## INTRODUCTION

This scenario is common for many university professors. At times, the content a faculty member teaches impacts the types of Student Evaluations of Teaching (SET) scores that will be received. For example, a professor of a difficult math class may consistently get lower SET scores from students who struggle with math content, or students may rate more lenient professors more favorably (Lawrence, 2018). According to the American Association of University Professors (AAUP), SET scores are not valid for evaluating teaching (Lawrence, 2018).

However, what about the professor who was unable to deliver content effectively? What if students did not learn content, or if grading seemed unfair? With student success a priority, knowledge about the role of assessment in education is critical. The purpose of this chapter is twofold. First of all, it is essential that faculty understand how to assess student learning; therefore, this chapter addresses ways to monitor student progress. A secondary purpose of this chapter is to address the evaluation of teaching effectiveness and the need for intentional reflection on our instructional practices. Since teaching effectiveness is a large part of a faculty evaluation, we will revisit Dr. Potter's dilemma and share the role of student and faculty evaluations.

## ACCOUNTABILITY AND ASSESSMENT

The assessment movement began in the mid-1980s (Ewell, 2009; National Institute for Learning Outcomes Assessment, 2019) and focused on the need for transparent information about student and institutional performance. Therefore, institutional assessment in higher education is essential to meet the requirements of regional accreditation in the United States (Provezis, 2010). Since the release of the Spellings Report (Spellings, 2006) and the Reauthorization of the Higher Education Act (Higher Education Opportunity Act, 2008), attention has been given to the expectation that regional accreditation organizations ensure high-quality education (Provezis, 2010). Therefore, institutions prioritize the collection and use of student learning outcomes and assessment data (Ewell, 2009; National Institute for Learning Outcomes Assessment, 2019) for strategic decision-making, curricula updates, and the improvement of student learning experiences. On your campus, you will observe assessment of institutional effectiveness, program assessment, and course level assessment. While it is essential for new faculty to understand the "big picture" of university-wide assessment, in this chapter, we focus on on course level assessment.

## THE ROLE OF OUTCOMES-BASED TEACHING, LEARNING, AND ASSESSMENT

The word assessment comes from the Latin word *assidere*, which means "to sit beside" (Online Etymology Dictionary, n.d., para. 2). Imagine the possibilities if we take this definition of assessment to heart and consider collaborating side-by-side with students to improve learning. Wiggins and McTighe (2006) define assessment as "the act of determining the extent to which the desired results are on the way to being achieved and to what extent they have been achieved" (p. 146). In Chapter 2, we defined outcomes-based teaching and learning based on Spady's (1994) work and practiced writing course learning outcomes. Since a CLO focuses on what students learn rather than what they are taught, much thought goes into the role of assessment and the evidence that tells us whether or not our students have achieved the desired results (Wiggins & McTighe, 2011). According to Wiggins and McTighe (2005), teachers first identify outcomes, they determine acceptable evidence to support those outcomes, then they plan corresponding instruction, tasks, and experiences. Referred to as backward design (Wiggins & McTighe, 2011), the idea is that educators have to consider the evidence to determine whether or not learning objectives were achieved. How do we measure knowledge and skills?

Wiggins and McTighe (2005) acknowledge that backward design may not come easily to teachers. They describe assessment as "more like a scrapbook of mementos and pictures than a single snapshot" (p. 152). They urge teachers to consider a variety of methods and formats for collecting evidence. We realize this may be more practical for teachers with smaller class sizes. However, there are ways for all professors to apply ongoing assessment through both formative and summative assessment practices.

## Formative Assessment

Formative assessments reveal students' understanding and misunderstanding through low-stakes assessment (Wiggins & McTighe, 2005). Formative assessments provide the teacher with ways to modify teaching and learning to help students improve. They also provide students with feedback that informs possible learning gaps as well as potential support resources they may need (Stanford, n.d.). Formative assessment may include entry and exit slips, questioning strategies, observations and more. An exit slip or exit ticket, for instance, is traditionally a written response students provide at the end of a lesson or lecture that assesses student understanding of material covered. For large classes or for online classes, an "exit ticket" may take the form of an online survey, which poses a question or two about the content and then provides immediate feedback for the student as well as data for the teacher to examine upon receipt.

## Summative Assessment

Summative assessments reveal the skills and knowledge a student has gained over the entire instructional period and provide data on student performance related to the learning goals of the course. Summative assessments are formal assessments used to provide the teacher with a measure of student performance. Summative assessments, if designed appropriately, based on CLOs, help students to understand how far they have come in meeting the learning goals of the course, what they need to work on, and what they should study next. Examples of summative assessments include exams, final projects, essays, and portfolios (and more). Some of these examples include assessments that might provide quantitative data. Others, like portfolios, provide qualitative data. In the next section, we will cover the basics of assessments.

## THE BASICS

Assessments should be aligned with learning objectives. Quantitative assessment provides numerical data relating to student learning. For instance, traditional assessment methods like examinations are useful for evaluating student learning in terms of remembering information and understanding and applying concepts and ideas. However, other forms of assessments may be more appropriate for evaluating how well students analyze, evaluate, or create products related to what they have learned. Qualitative assessments, such as presentations, field experiences, project planning and management, may provide insight into student application of content. It may be tempting to assess skills easiest to test and grade, but alignment to learning outcomes is key. We address additional assessment options in the next sections.

## Qualitative Assessments

In some ways, it has become easier to develop assessments for our classrooms. We use generative AI to help us with assessment ideas and assessment examples. The thing to remember about AI, though, is that our students are using it, too. Therefore, educators must become familiar with the outputs AI tools can generate, such as essays, reflections, or summaries. The design of your assessments may need to circumvent student use of these tools. Another option would be to clarify expectations of AI use, including what is permissible and what is not. Qualitative assessments designed for originality prove most useful. For example, you might have your students write personal reflections or connect to authentic experiences. You might have students respond to local or course-specific prompts or analyze class discussions or non-digital resources. The use of prompts that ask students to synthesize multiple perspectives or argue from a unique position may prevent undesirable use of AI tools.

### Performance Assessments

One type of qualitative assessment, performance assessments, requires students to apply their learning to a new and authentic situation as means of assessing their understanding and ability to transfer their learning (Wiggins & McTighe, 2005). For example, a performance task for an education major might be to develop and deliver a phonics lesson. Table 3.1 provides examples of performance assessments across a variety of disciplines.

*Table 3.1* Performance Assessment Examples

| Discipline | Example |
| --- | --- |
| Education | Lesson plan and delivery |
| Business | SWOT (Strengths, Weaknesses, Opportunities, Threats) analysis and strategic plan |
| Sociology | Social issue (research-/evidence-based solution) |
| Math | Product design (analyze and optimize the design of a product to improve its efficiency in terms of materials and cost) |
| English | Text analysis and adaptation (analyze a literary work, synthesize critical insights, and creatively adapt the text for a modern audience while maintaining its core themes and message) |

Authentic tasks like those shared in Table 3.1 present the learner with a real-world problem. Real-world problems are not multiple-choice, so implementing these types of tasks requires students to apply knowledge and skills they have learned.

## *Presentations*

Presentations are qualitative tasks in which students teach others what they have learned. Presentations typically require students to communicate content by presenting visual materials and interacting with their audience.

## *Projects*

Student projects result in a product students create, such as a plan, document, artifact, or object. Projects can be completed individually or in groups. They typically span a sustained period of time and enable students to demonstrate skills or understanding of the topic of learning.

## *Portfolios*

Portfolios include a collection of documents, objects, and artifacts collected and curated by students to demonstrate their learning over a wide range of learning goals. Portfolios usually include students' reflections of their own learning. Portfolios are typically completed over a span of time and are usually done by individual students as opposed to groups.

## **Grading**

Another key component of assessment is the evaluation of student work. Teachers need a standardized and equitable way to assess student learning to communicate student achievement. When planning ways to evaluate student work, consider the class size and the content. Some assessments include right or wrong answers that are easy to grade. Some assignments, like the qualitative assignments we described, require you to spend time planning and developing assessment tools, like rubrics.

## **Rubrics**

Consider the use of rubrics to promote fair and consistent grading processes. Rubrics are "criterion-referenced grading tools that describe qualitative differences in student performance for evaluating and scoring assessments" (Messier, 2022, para. 1). A rubric usually resembles a table or matrix and presents a set of performance criteria along with a rating scale and indicators for the different rating scores. Rubrics help ensure consistency of assessment across different students, contributing to fair grading. Rubrics also can make grading more efficient and help to create consistency between multiple graders and across assignments. Not only is a rubric helpful to the grader, students benefit from access to rubrics

## Christian Studies Assignment: Biblical Themes in Modern Life

**Assignment Overview**

Choose a key biblical theme (e.g., forgiveness, justice, faith, servant leadership, grace) and write a **one-page reflection** on how this theme applies to a modern situation or personal experience. Use at least one Bible verse to support your analysis.

**Guiding Questions:**

- What is the biblical theme you are discussing?
- How does Scripture define or exemplify this theme?
- How can this theme be applied to a real-world situation or personal experience?
- What insights does this theme provide for Christian living today?

**Grading Rubric (20 Points Total)**

| Criteria | Excellent (5) | Good (4) | Satisfactory (3) | Needs Improvement (1-2) |
|---|---|---|---|---|
| Clarity & Focus | Clear, well-organized reflection with strong central theme | Mostly clear with minor organization issues | Somewhat unclear or lacks focus | Lacks clarity and coherence |
| Biblical Support | Strong use of Scripture with clear connection to theme | Uses Scripture effectively but lacks depth | Uses Scripture but connection is weak | Little or no biblical support |
| Application | Insightful and relevant real-world application | Mostly relevant but could be more developed | Application is vague or somewhat unclear | Lacks meaningful application |
| Grammar & Writing | Well-written with no errors | Minor grammar issues but readable | Noticeable errors that affect readability | Many errors that distract from meaning |

*Figure 3.1* AI-Generated Assignment and Rubric
OpenAI. (2025). ChatGPT [Large language model. https://chatgpt.com

so they can understand the assignment expectations from the start, ensuring transparency with students on exactly what is being assessed. Developing rubrics has become easier with AI tools. The assignment and rubric in Figure 3.1 was developed by ChatGPT. Another source for rubric development is Rubistar.com, which includes many premade rubrics for use as well as templates you can use to build your own.

## Constructive Feedback

In addition to grades, students need general and constructive feedback. Consider ways to offer timely and detailed feedback that helps learners understand their strengths and areas for improvement. Feedback on discussion board posts may be a way to connect with students in online courses. Verbal and written feedback should be provided on graded assignments. Students benefit from detailed explanations of point deductions on assignments. Highlight specific examples from their work to illustrate key points.

## BEYOND THE BASICS

Now that we have examined ways to assess student performance, we transition to the concept of assessing teaching effectiveness. Faculty evaluate student performance, and students traditionally have the opportunity to evaluate *our* performance. Student ratings of performance on the internet can be an interesting read. Spend time reading reviews on "Rate My Professor" and you will quickly understand our discomfort with this topic. Comments like "He is a great teacher but not an okay person" and "avoid him if you can he is through with student" cause immediate alarm. In this section, we consider a variety of ways to assess teaching effectiveness. We begin by addressing the SET.

### Student Feedback in Higher Education

Student feedback regarding faculty performance in higher education has become a standard part of a university teacher's job (Flodén, 2017). Instructors like Dr. Potter become discouraged upon reading SETs, especially when they have spent a great deal of time and effort planning for student success. Flodén (2017) investigated 75 teachers' perceptions of student feedback and how it influences the instructional decisions made by the teacher in higher education. The study found that student feedback was perceived positively by the university teachers, had a large impact on their teaching, and helped improve courses. However, teachers receiving negative student feedback, who were often less experienced, reported more negative feelings and were more likely to introduce unjustified changes to their teaching in order to please students. Additional, evidence-based practices can be put into place that may help improve SET (Flodén, 2017). In the next few sections, we provide ways to understand and address students' concerns using various forms of feedback.

### SET

Even though Dr. Potter experienced negative student feedback, he should reflect on student evaluations. Few students commented, but those responses may be beneficial. For example, a few students remarked on the fast pacing of lectures, so he might consider slowing down or pausing between topics. The other comments related to his assessments. Students commented that they understood the content but did poorly on his multiple-choice quizzes and exams. Dr. Potter could address this feedback in several ways, including the implementation of alternative assessment methods to gain a more comprehensive understanding of students' strengths and weaknesses. Instead of complete reliance on multiple-choice assessments, he could include test items that require students show their work and explain their reasoning. Another alternative might include problem-based applications of the course content, in which students solve real-world math applications.

Positive comments offer insight into student needs as well. When students comment about good teaching but follow it up with a comment about too much work, that is not a bad evaluation. Students need to engage in learning outside of class, and too much work may indicate that the class was a challenge. The *type* of work is important, but when a student notes good teaching, that constitutes a win. Dr. Gonzales should track any changes he makes to address comments, as the narrative of change and growth needs to be documented.

## Collect Additional Feedback

Collecting feedback at the beginning of the semester may help you understand students' expectations or, depending on the class size, could help you become better acquainted with your students (Stanford, n.d.). Whether gathering feedback through discussions or using digital tools, provide class time for feedback to ensure they share. In addition, we recommend you address feedback sooner rather than later.

Midway through the semester, it is recommended you seek specific feedback regarding student learning (Stanford, n.d.). For example, you might develop a survey that asks students what is working well for them or if they could suggest specific examples of changes that might improve the course. Obtaining preliminary ratings on the course provides you with the opportunity to address any concerns students have and demonstrates your efforts toward student success. It is appropriate to discuss the suggestions you will implement and why as well as those you will not implement (and why). In the case that students mention you go too fast or that they get confused, encourage the class to ask questions during class.

Formative assessments, as described above, should guide your instruction. If students perform poorly on an exit ticket, for instance, you will want to reteach material or provide resources for students to study. Talk to students about the support they need and work to provide it. Student learning is our goal!

## Assessing and Improving Teaching Effectiveness

From a university perspective, positive feedback is reflective of good teaching. However, many studies reveal otherwise. For decades, research has indicated gender and racial bias in student evaluations (Doerer, 2019). In addition, an overemphasis on student evaluations could result in grade inflation and potentially harm student learning (Vasey & Carroll, 2016). For example, one study found that students who take a prerequisite class with high SET that students were likely to do worse in the second class. Students are customers and deserve a voice. The question has become, how much impact should that voice have on faculty evaluations of teaching effectiveness? Some colleges have reconsidered the role SET play in faculty members' careers, seeking alternative ways to define teaching excellence (Doerer, 2019), including some of the examples in the following section.

## *Observations*

Some universities have implemented peer observations, in which colleagues are asked to evaluate instructors' teaching by observing classes, reviewing course materials, and considering instructors' written reflections (Doerer, 2019). The peer feedback process at our university is voluntary but definitely beneficial. Our form includes a place for observation notes and comments concerning class preparation, atmosphere, presentation and delivery of the lesson, strengths of the instruction, and possible suggests for lesson enhancement. Finally, the form provides a space for a summative commentary concerning teaching effectiveness. Because we are trained as educators, it is common for us to have faculty from other disciplines observe our classrooms to gain insight into teaching practices that may differ from traditional practices.

In addition to peer observations, deans and associate deans may observe classes to provide feedback regarding teaching effectiveness. Peers or administrators can visit classrooms or review an online course for appropriate structure and resources. It is important to remember that one observation provides just a snapshot of a teacher's performance.

## *Self-Reflection*

Professors analyze their own teaching through self-reflection. Kirpalani (2017) examined self-reflective practices for faculty in higher education as a way to improve teaching effectiveness. Professors can reflect on several aspects, or "knowledge domains of teaching, including instruction, pedagogical, and curricular knowledge. Reflection can include asking yourself questions about your instruction and delivery. It can also include recording and analyzing classroom sessions to identify areas for improvement. Review your online course design for accessibility. Frameworks such as Quality Matters standards help ensure clear learning objectives, organized content, a positive online culture, and access to content and processes.

## Teaching Portfolios

Teaching effectiveness may be demonstrated through a collection of artifacts. Teaching portfolios represent your identity as a teacher (DePaul, n.d.). A teaching portfolio may include a list of courses taught, syllabi, lesson plans, descriptions of in-class activities, assessments, summarized student evaluations (including notes from students) and examples of student work. This practice may benefit tenure-track professors as they develop their portfolio for the tenure and promotion process. It enables professionals to reflect on instructional methods and to track teaching growth over time (DePaul, n.d.).

## Professional Development

Many colleges have built-in resources to improve teaching effectiveness, including professional development (PD) opportunities. Take advantage of centers for teaching and learning and PD offered for faculty. We use our center and frequent PD offerings, which have recently included PD on technology applications like AI and Microsoft Teams. In addition to easily accessible PD on our campus, consider attending conferences that focus on teaching effectiveness.

# SELF-MENTORSHIP

Assessment includes the collection and analysis of data. Reflecting on and using data to inform decisions, based on evidence, provides an ideal way to improve teaching and learning. In this chapter, you learned about the role of assessment in outcomes-based teaching and learning. In addition, you read about foundational assessment concepts, such as summative and formative assessments, as ways to assess student learning. The use of student feedback offers additional ways to improve teaching, even when the feedback is disappointing, like the feedback Dr. Potter received. Consider a variety of strategies, like peer observations, self-reflection, and teaching portfolios to obtain as much feedback for growth as possible.

Assessment is a complex topic. Through the practice of self-mentorship, you will develop your own personal and professional growth by seeking ways to assess student learning. Our Mentoring Moment exercises for this chapter (Exercises 3.1-3.3) prompt you to develop assessments and rubrics as well as an exit ticket using Google Forms. You are also ready to work on your first syllabus, now that you understand the connection between outcomes and assessment. We have provided a template for you to use as you outline your course.

# REFERENCES

DePaul. (n.d.). Teaching portfolios. Teaching Commons. https://resources.depaul.edu/teaching-commons/teaching-guides/reflective-practice/Pages/teaching-portfolios.aspx

Doerer, K. (an. 13, 2019). Colleges are getting smarter about student evlautions. Here's how. The Chronicle of Higher Education. https://www.chronicle.com/article/colleges-are-getting-smarter-about-student-evaluations-heres-how/

Ewell, P. T. (Nov., 2009). Assessment, accountability, and improvement: Revisiting the tension. (Occasional Paper No. 1). Urbana, IL: University of Illinois and Indiana University, National Institute for Learning Outcomes Assessment (NILOA). https://www.learningoutcomesassessment.org/wp-content/uploads/2019/02/OccasionalPaper1.pdf

Flodén, F. (2017). The impact of student feedback on teaching in higher education. Assessment & Evlauation in Higher Education, 42(7),1054–1068. https://doi.org/10.1080/02602938.2016.1224997

The Higher Education Opportunity Act (2008). Pub. L. 110–315. *Stat. 3078* (2008). https://www.govinfo.gov/content/pkg/PLAW-110publ315/pdf/PLAW-110publ315.pdf

Kirpalani, N. (2017). Developing self-reflective practices to improve teaching effectiveness. *Journal of Higher Education Theory and Practice, 17*(8), 73–80. https://research-ebsco-com.dewey.umhb.edu/linkprocessor/plink?id=1e2a7e08-db72-3c13-8226-c45d0d135f64

Lawrence, J. W. (2018). Student evaluations of teaching are not valid. American Association of University Professors. https://www.aaup.org/article/student-evaluations-teaching-are-not-valid#:~:text=The%20researchers%20also%20reviewed%20two,anticipate%20earning%20a%20high%20grade

Messier, N. (June 28, 2022). Rubrics. University of Illinois Chicago. https://teaching.uic.edu/cate-teaching-guides/assessment-grading-practices/rubrics/

National Institute for Learning Outcomes Assessment. (2019, January). A historical overview of assessment: 1980s-2000s (Assessment Brief). Urbana, IL: University of Illinois and Indiana University, National Institute for Learning Outcomes Assessment (NILOA)

Online Etymology Dictionary. Assessment. https://www.etymonline.com/word/assessment

Provezis, S. (Oct., 2010). Regional accreditation and student learning outcomes: Mapping the territory. (Occasional Paper No. 6). University of Illinois and Indiana University, National Institute for Learning Outcomes Assessment (NILOA). https://www.learningoutcomesassessment.org/wp-content/uploads/2019/02/OccasionalPaper6.pdf

Spady W. G. (1994). *Outcome-based education: Critical issues and answers*. Arlington, VA: American Association of School Administrators.

Spellings, M. (2006). A test of leadership: Charting the future of U.S. higher education." [Report]. U.S. Department of Education. https://files.eric.ed.gov/fulltext/ED493504.pdf

Stanford University (n.d.). Course planning. https://teachingcommons.stanford.edu/teaching-guides/foundations-course-design/course-planning

Vasey, C., & Carroll, L. (2016). How do we evaluation teaching? American Association of University Professors. https://www.aaup.org/article/how-do-we-evaluate-teaching#.WrFBzOgbNPY%0A

Wiggins, G., & McTighe, J. (2011). *The Understanding by Design guide to creating high-quality units*. ASCD.

Wiggins, G., & McTighe, J. (2005). Understanding by design, 2$^{nd}$ edition. Association for Supervision and Curriculum Development.

# Section I:
# Teaching Effectiveness

## INTRODUCTION: EXERCISE 0.1
### Why?

In this exercise, reflect on the following question: Why become a college professor?

# INTRODUCTION: EXERCISE 0.2

| K | W | L |
|---|---|---|

Teaching Excellence

Scholarship

Service

## CHAPTER 1: EXERCISE 1.1

### Building Relationships

Plan two ice breaker activities you could use with one of your f2f classes, and plan two ice breaker activities you could use with one of your online classes. Ice breakers can be easily found online, but consider asking a generative AI tool for some ideas.

Generative AI tools to try: ChatGPT (https://chatgpt.com/), Gemini (https://gemini.google.com/app); MagicSchoolAI (https://www.magicschool.ai/)

Fill in your ideas:

Ice Breaker #1 (f2f)


Ice Breaker #2 (f2f)


Ice Breaker #3 (online)


Ice Breaker #4 (online)

## CHAPTER 1: EXERCISE 1.2

Use the information chapter 1 to determine if high-impact practices (HIP) would align with your program or courses. Are there any you could incorporate into your classes?

| High-Impact Practice | Course Connection |
|---|---|
| | |
| | |
| | |
| | |
| | |

# CHAPTER 1: EXERCISE 1.3

## Technology Tools for Teaching

Try some of the technology tools commonly used in college classrooms. Write a description of the tool so you can revisit it for future applications.

| Technology Tool | Description | Application |
|---|---|---|
| Kahoot | | |
| Blooket | | |
| PollEverywhere.com | | |
| AI | | |
| Padlet | | |
| Google Forms | | |
| EDPuzzle | | |
| Pear Deck | | |
| NearPod | | |
| Zoom, Teams, etc. (try a new one) | | |
| Flip | | |
| **Accessibility Tools** | | |
| Captions on Slides | | |
| Read Aloud Feature in Word | | |

## CHAPTER 2: EXERCISE 2.1
### Teaching Philosophy

Write a teaching philosophy statement based on your foundational beliefs about effective teaching. What are your views on student engagement and student learning? How does research inform your teaching?

### Getting Started:

Brainstorm ideas below. On the next page, begin drafting your statement.

Statement of Teaching Philosophy:

## CHAPTER 2: EXERCISE 2.2
### Writing Learning Outcomes

For this exercise, choose a class. Then write down that you want students to know and be able to do as a result of this course.

| Class | Know and Be Able to Do |
|---|---|
|   |   |
|   |   |
|   |   |

Now, construct learning outcomes using this model from Stanford Teaching Commons:

They use an ABCD strategy. A is for audience; B is for behavior; C is for condition; D is for degree. Here is a sentence stem they provide as an example:

Students (audience) will be able to label and describe (behavior), given a diagram of the eye at the end of this lesson (condition), all seven extraocular muscles, and at least two of their actions (degree).

Tip: Before writing your own learning outcomes, we encourage you to refresh your memory on Blooms Taxonomy to inspire verb choice.

Create your own learning outcomes:

### Resources for This Exercise:

National Institute for Learning Outcomes Assessment: https://learningoutcomesassessment.org

Stanford Teaching Commons: https://www.Teachingcommons.stanford.edu

## CHAPTER 2: EXERCISE 2.3
## Course Content

In this mentoring moment, we ask you to consider your course content. Start by researching textbooks and other resources that align with your course and support the learning outcomes you created in Exercise 2. See if you can find any resources in Creative Commons content that would be free to use: https://search.creativecommons.org/

| Resource | Cost to Student | Rating (Rate Quality from 1–5) |
|---|---|---|
| | | |
| | | |
| | | |
| | | |
| | | |

# CHAPTER 3: EXERCISE 3.1

## Rubrics

There are many ways to create rubrics. You will find an example, created with the help of OpenAI. Use the example to create a rubric for one of the major assignments in a class of your choosing.

## Rubric Template

Assignment: _____
Student Name: _____
Date: _____

| Criteria | Excellent (4) | Proficient (3) | Developing (2) | Needs Improvement (1) | Score |
|---|---|---|---|---|---|
| Understanding & Analysis | Demonstrates deep understanding with insightful analysis | Shows good understanding with clear analysis | Demonstrates partial understanding with some analysis | Limited understanding with minimal or unclear analysis | ___ |
| Organization & Structure | Well-organized, logical flow, and clear transitions | Mostly well-organized, minor structural issues | Some organization, but ideas may be unclear | Lacks organization, difficult to follow | ___ |
| Evidence & Support | Strong, relevant evidence with excellent integration | Adequate evidence with good integration | Limited or weak evidence, partially integrated | Little to no evidence or integration | ___ |
| Clarity & Writing Quality | Clear, concise, and well-written with minimal errors | Mostly clear with a few errors | Somewhat unclear with multiple errors | Lacks clarity, frequent errors | ___ |
| Engagement & Originality | Highly engaging and original ideas | Engaging with some originality | Some originality, but limited engagement | Lacks originality and engagement | ___ |

**Total Score:** ____ / 20
**Comments:**

OpenAI. (2025). *ChatGPT* [Large language model]. https://chatgpt.com

## CHAPTER 3: EXERCISE 3.2
### Creating an Exit Ticket

Google forms are a great tool for conducting an informal assessment. For this assignment we challenge you to create an exit ticket for a class. We provide the following as an example for use in a research class:

1. Name

2. What insight did you gain as a result of today's class session?

3. How does today's class session content connect to the theoretical framework you selected for your research?

4. On a scale of 1–5, rate your confidence in applying your learning to your research
   Not Confident   Somewhat Confident   Neutral   Confident   Very Confident

Create your own exit ticket! Use the space below for your ideas:

_____
_____
_____
_____
_____
_____
_____
_____
_____

## CHAPTER 3: EXERCISE 3.3

### Syllabus Template

The following are standard items to include on a syllabus. You can use this to create your syllabus. We like to give our students a semester calendar. Now, we tell them that the calendar can change to meet student learning needs. Students appreciate being able to see when major assignments are due so that they can plan ahead.

### Contact Information

Instructor:
Office Phone:
Cell Phone:
E-mail:
Office Hours:

### Description of the Course

Course Name, Number and Section:
Term:
Catalog Description:
Time/Location Course Meets:
Course Objectives:
Required Textbook(s):
Mode of Delivery and Credit Hour Description:
Academic Honesty:
AI Use Policy:
Grading and Assignments (see schedule for due dates):
Grading Policies:
Grading Scale:
Academic Decorum:
Attendance Policy:

## Schedule of Course Activities

The schedule of activities is tentative and may be modified based on class need. Any changes to the schedule will be posted on the learning management system in advance and discussed in class before due dates.

| Date | Content |
| --- | --- |
|  |  |
|  |  |
|  |  |
|  |  |
|  |  |
|  |  |
|  |  |
|  |  |
|  |  |

# Part II
Research and Scholarship

## Chapter 4

# What Is Scholarship?

**FACULTY FOCUS**

*Dr. Takeisha Lewis, a recent addition to the Business Department at a four-year institution, is eager to begin her academic career but feels lost when it comes to scholarship. Although she is knowledgeable in her field, she is new to academia and unsure how to initiate her research and publishing. Dr. Lewis is unclear about what research topics would be valued by her department and how to align her interests with departmental expectations. With no experience in academic publishing beyond her dissertation, Dr. Lewis finds the process overwhelming and doesn't know which journals or conferences are respected in her discipline. She fears that asking for guidance might reveal her inexperience, potentially harming her professional image. As her first year progresses without any scholarly accomplishments, her anxiety about her lack of research output grows. This stress is beginning to impact her confidence, making the idea of starting her research even more intimidating. Dr. Lewis worries that she is falling behind, especially since scholarship is crucial for her future evaluations.*

**INTRODUCTION**

The transition to the role of faculty comes with a learning curve. Coming from a K-12 background, my days were structured for me with very little flexibility. When I (Brenda) was preparing to interview for my first academic position, I spoke with a trusted friend and former professor at the university. I asked about her hours and what a typical day and week looked like for her. She quickly pointed out that what she does may not be considered typical; she worked significantly more than 40 hours. I could not wrap my head around where all of those hours came from. My load would be 24 credits in an academic year in a schedule that appeared to be much less than my high school English job. I clearly had a lot to learn! The first semester of my academic career quickly cleared up my confusion on where the hours went.

DOI: 10.4324/9781003484196-8

My experience is not unique. The role of the university professor has continued to expand, requiring professors to allocate time to a number of initiatives, committee work, department needs, etc. It is no wonder that at the end of the day or work week, professors are tired. Yes, we enjoy flexible schedules, however, as Berg and Seeber pointed out in *The Slow Professor*, "while flexibility of hours is one of the privileges of our work, it can easily translate into working all the time or feeling that one should" (2017, p. 16). This statement reflects why faculty can have a difficult time factoring scholarship into the mix. Where does one begin with scholarship? How is scholarship defined?

The purpose of this chapter is to provide an overview of multiple types of scholarship through several perspectives and models. This chapter begins with a short summary of the history of research as scholarship to provide context for how research was defined. We then consider the work of Ernest Boyer, who expanded the traditional definition of research, as well as others who challenge us to consider public and collaborative work as scholarship.

## HISTORICAL PERSPECTIVE

American colleges and universities were founded in the late 1630's to provide education through a "collegiate tradition brought to colonial America from England" (Glassik et al., 1997, p. 6). This model focused on teaching as the primary responsibility of the college professor. However, as the nation grew, so did the need for an educated workforce, including inventors, innovators, and creative individuals able to problem-solve. The Morrill Act of 1862 created "land-grant colleges", which connected universities to the needs of the developing nation (Glassik et al., 1997, p. 7), creating a partnership between higher education learning and the needs of the community, state, and nation. Over the next few decades, scholars who had earned post-graduate degrees in Europe brought their experiences back to the United States, which expanded the educational focus to now include graduate students with programs that engaged in research (Glassik et al., 1997), launching a path of discovery. As newly minted Ph.D. scholars joined colleges and universities, they chose to engage in original research through discovery. Their research activities influenced others to follow suit, and people also moved from institution to institution, carrying with them this new model of faculty as researchers. "Research as a model for faculty work then began to spread exponentially and to colonize the academy as a whole" (Glassik et al., 1997, p. 7). At first, only a few individuals engaged in discovery, but it soon became the expectation of all faculty. Glassik et al. (1997) described this as a "pervasive transformation of faculty priorities in American higher education" (p. 7).

Research brought notoriety and prestige to higher education institutions and with it outside funding through grants. Faculty members who engaged in high-profile research grants were sought-after. Promotion and tenure criteria began to rely more on publications and research activities than before. It was clear—faculty engaged in research were rewarded. A 1993 study by Fairweather found that, regardless of institution type or focus, a research model had emerged. Unfortunately, this model did not provide flexibility for faculty to engage in ways that met their discipline's or individual strengths and still be deemed research or scholarship by their institutions. Acknowledging that this definition was too narrow, Ernest Boyer proposed an expanded definition of scholarship in 1990. This opened new pathways for faculty to engage in scholarly activities and have their work honored.

## SCHOLARSHIP RECONSIDERED

Ernest Boyer (1990) pointed out that "scholarship in earlier times referred to a variety of creative work carried on in a variety of places, and its integrity was measured by the ability to think, communicate, and learn" (Boyer, 1990, p. 15). Boyer then proceeded to boldly consider new definitions of the work of faculty to be more inclusive of the complexities of the role, thereby expanding ways in which faculty work within this new definition and how that work is evaluated. "There is a recognition that the faculty reward system does not match the full range of academic functions and that professors are often caught between competing obligations" (Boyer, 1990, p. 1). In order to alleviate the mismatch, Boyer suggested America's colleges and universities consider a new vision of scholarship better aligned with clear campus missions and the work of academic institutions. This alignment would be consistent with the realities of increasingly diverse institutions of higher education. Boyer's goal was to broaden traditional views of scholarship in ways that leveraged faculty talent. The redefining of scholarship had to be more flexible to be applicable to all academic disciplines (Boyer, 1990). He proposed four categories: scholarship of *discovery*; scholarship of *integration*; scholarship of *application*; and scholarship of *teaching*.

### Discovery

Boyer (1990) defined this category as the most traditional or most similar to the long-standing definition of research. It "contributes not only to the stock of human knowledge but also to the intellectual climate of a college or university" (p. 17). Discovery enhances both the collective body of human knowledge and the intellectual environment of a college or university (Nibert, 2001).

### *Examples of the Scholarship of Discovery*

#### Example 1:

Dr. Elizabeth Lang, a seasoned nursing professor, was deeply concerned about the rising rates of burnout among nurses. Inspired by the growing body of research on mindfulness meditation, she embarked on a groundbreaking study to investigate its potential benefits for healthcare professionals.

Dr. Lang's research involved a rigorous randomized controlled trial. She recruited a diverse group of nurses from various clinical settings and randomly assigned them to either a mindfulness meditation group or a control group. The mindfulness group participated in weekly mindfulness meditation sessions, guided by experienced instructors. The control group received standard care.

Over the course of several months, Dr. Lang and her team collected data on participants' stress levels, job satisfaction, and physical health outcomes. They used a variety of measures, including self-report questionnaires, physiological assessments, and clinical records.

As the study progressed, Dr. Lang was eager to analyze the results. She was particularly interested in whether mindfulness meditation could reduce stress, improve job satisfaction, and enhance nurses' overall well-being. Her findings had the potential to revolutionize the way healthcare organizations support their staff and promote a healthier work environment.

**Example 2:**

Dr. Watt, an experienced social work professor, was known for her unwavering commitment to social justice. Her research, deeply rooted in the scholarship of discovery, often delved into the lives of marginalized communities. Currently, she was immersed in a project examining the impact of gentrification on low-income families in urban neighborhoods.

Dr. Watt spent countless hours conducting in-depth interviews with residents, observing community dynamics, and analyzing historical data. Her research uncovered a complex interplay of factors contributing to displacement, including rising housing costs, changing demographics, and discriminatory housing practices. She was particularly interested in the experiences of families of color, who were disproportionately affected by these trends.

Through her research, Dr. Watt aimed to illuminate the hidden costs of gentrification and advocate for policies that promote equitable development. She believed that by understanding the lived experiences of marginalized communities, she could empower them to shape their own futures. Her work was not merely academic; it had the potential to inform social policy and inspire community-based interventions.

## Integration

This scholarship category is meant for scholars who "give meaning to isolated facts" (p. 18) and situate those facts into context or viewpoint. The focus is on multidisciplinary connections. Boyer defined this as "serious, disciplined work that seeks to interpret, draw together, and bring new insight to bear on original research" (p. 19). It encourages scholars to engage in conversations, find connections, and collaborate with others in disciplinary fields that are not their own. Boyer placed importance on the rapid change within society that call for conversations between experts from different backgrounds.

## Examples of the Scholarship of Integration

### Example 1:

Dr. Smith, a history professor, was intrigued by the intersection of history and technology. She initiated a digital humanities project to create interactive timelines and virtual tours of historic sites. By combining historical research with cutting-edge technology, Dr. Smith was able to bring history to life for a wider audience.

Her project involved collaborating with computer science students, historians, and museum curators. Together, they developed innovative tools and techniques to engage learners of all ages. This interdisciplinary approach not only enriched the historical narrative but also fostered new collaborations and knowledge exchange across different disciplines.

### Example 2:

Dr. Maya Patel, a sociologist, was fascinated by the intersection of technology and social relationships. While her research focused on the impact of social media on adolescent mental health, she realized that a broader, interdisciplinary perspective was needed to fully understand the complex dynamics at play.

She partnered with a psychologist, Dr. Ethan Lee, who specialized in adolescent development. Together, they designed a research project that combined qualitative and quantitative methods to explore how social media use influenced teenagers' self-esteem, social interactions, and overall well-being.

Dr. Patel and Dr. Lee collaborated closely, sharing their expertise and insights. They conducted in-depth interviews with adolescents, analyzed social media data, and administered psychological assessments. By integrating their diverse perspectives, they were able to uncover nuanced patterns and develop a more comprehensive understanding of the phenomenon.

Their research findings challenged conventional wisdom and highlighted the need for a nuanced approach to addressing the impact of technology on young people. Their work not only advanced the field of sociology but also had significant implications for mental health professionals, educators, and policymakers.

## Application

This type of scholarship engages the scholar in applying knowledge. Questions that guide this category include, "How can knowledge be responsibly applied to consequential problems? How can it be helpful to individuals as well as institutions?" and further, "Can social problems *themselves* define an agenda for scholarly investigation?" (Boyer, 1990, p. 21). This scholarship can contribute to new knowledge if there is attention given to both theory and practice (Boyer, 1990). Scholarship of Application is innovation based on new knowledge to address issues within society.

## *Examples of the Scholarship of Application*

### Example 1:

Dr. Nathan Peters, a clinical psychologist, was deeply concerned about the rising rates of adolescent depression and anxiety. He recognized the urgent need to translate psychological research into effective interventions for young people.

Dr. Peters developed a new cognitive-behavioral therapy (CBT) program specifically tailored to the needs of adolescents. This program incorporated mindfulness techniques, problem-solving skills, and social skills training. He conducted a randomized controlled trial to evaluate the effectiveness of this new intervention compared to standard care.

The results of the study were promising. Adolescents who received the CBT program showed significant improvements in their mental health symptoms, compared to those in the control group. Dr. Peters' research demonstrated the potential of evidence-based interventions to address the mental health needs of young people.

He didn't stop there. Dr. Peters worked closely with schools and community organizations to train teachers, counselors, and parents in the implementation of his CBT program. He developed user-friendly manuals and online resources to support the dissemination of his research findings.

Through his commitment to applying knowledge to real-world problems, Dr. Peters made a significant impact on the lives of young people struggling with mental health challenges. His work exemplifies the Scholarship of Application, bridging the gap between research and practice to create positive social change.

### Example 2:

Dr. Maria Ramirez, an environmental engineer, was passionate about finding sustainable solutions to global water scarcity. She combined her expertise in engineering with a deep understanding of social and economic factors to develop innovative water treatment technologies.

Dr. Ramirez worked closely with communities in rural areas of low-income countries to understand their specific water challenges and needs. She designed and implemented low-cost, community-based water filtration systems that could be easily maintained and operated by local residents.

By integrating engineering principles with community engagement and capacity building, Dr. Ramirez's research had a direct and lasting impact on improving access to clean water and promoting public health. Her work exemplifies the Scholarship of Application, demonstrating how knowledge can be applied to address critical global challenges.

## Teaching

Teaching is defined as scholarship due to the complex dance between the knowledge of the professor, transmission of knowledge and construction of knowledge between the two, through active participation. Faculty, as scholars, are lifelong learners in the quest for new knowledge to not only transmit knowledge, but transform and extend knowledge with and through their students (Boyer, 1990). This category is difficult to concisely define and assess. Glassick (2000) called it "elusive" in as much as it is complicated to distinguish between quality teaching and the scholarship of teaching (p. 879).

### *Examples of the Scholarship of Teaching*

#### Example 1:

As an educator concerned about students' abilities to evaluate online information, I (Jodi) have done considerable work in the field of digital literacy that fits into Boyer's teaching category. My job is to train future educators, so my research informs instruction, particularly in ways to teach young children about website features and online navigation. My work has been supported by several internal grants that have provided funding for technology tools and teacher training. In this example, I describe one of my first iPad projects titled, "Developing the Role of Technology in Literacy Education."

Internal grant funding from UMHB for a research project enabled me to purchase iPads for use in the College of Education. In an effort to promote technology integration, I needed to get technology into the hands of my future teachers. Keep in mind that iPads were a fairly new tool in 2012. Using these new iPads, the teaching and learning began. In the summer of 2012, our department hosted a "Technology Camp", which accompanied an education class I was teaching. The camp was designed for middle school students. Participants completed a questionnaire that collected information about topics they would like to learn about. We had topics ranging from gummy bears to Native Americans. Based on the questionnaire, each participant was paired with a UMHB student. Through a weeklong process of technology integration to teach a content area, I gained insight into ways to use the iPad in content area literacy instruction and published my findings in a journal published by the International Society for Technology in Education (ISTE).

Example 2:

Although I (Jodi) have many examples that relate to the field of education, I can also share one that could fit in any field of study—AI. Of course I studied AI's impact on classroom practices, but anyone could take AI and study its impact on their own field, especially the impact of AI in the higher education classroom. AI has changed the way we teach and the way we assess our college students. If we assign a paper, we question the authenticity of the paper due to the accessibility of AI. Again, using grant funding, I sought training on AI through ISTE University and I purchased literature to study. Through my ISTE training, I learned about a website called https://teachablemachine.withgoogle.com/ that I could use to teach future educators how AI works and to demonstrate how to use it to reinforce phonics skills in young children. I used the website to train the machine to recognize short a and long a sounds. Then I submitted a proposal to present this topic at a practitioners' session at the national conference of the Association of Literacy Educators and Research. Through the research process, I learned how to improve my pedagogical practices.

## Community-Engaged Scholarship

Another model of scholarship is that of Community-Engaged Scholarship (CES). The Carnegie Classification of Institutions of Higher Education defines CES as:

Community engagement describes collaboration between institutions of higher education and their larger communities (local, regional/state, national, global) for the mutually beneficial exchange of knowledge and resources in a context of partnership and reciprocity. The purpose of community engagement is the partnership of college and university knowledge and resources with those of the public and private sectors to enrich scholarship, research, and creative activity; enhance curriculum, teaching, and learning; prepare educated, engaged citizens; strengthen democratic values and civic responsibility; address critical societal issues; and contribute to the public good. (Carnegie Classification of Institutions of Higher Education, n.d., para 1.)

This type of scholarship "validates the knowledge assets of individuals outside the academy" (Janke, et al., 2023, p. 52). It does not rely merely on the knowledge of the academy but joins academic knowledge with community partners, forming a mutually beneficial relationship (Nicotera, et al., 2022). The scholarship that emerges goes beyond long-established peer-reviewed publications or grant work, and honors diverse scholarly activities by providing an expanded definition of what qualifies as scholarship (Nicotera, et al., 2022). The foundations of CES is entrenched in "inclusivity, equity, and social justice" (Jenke et al., 2023, p. 52).

CES has gained popularity in recent years with a new group of scholars (Post et al., 2016), which includes "underrepresented faculty—faculty of color and women" (Jenke et al., 2023, p. 52). While more faculty are finding their place in CES, a hinderance to engaging in CES is its' lack of inclusion in institutional scholarship definitions (O'Meara, 2015), leading to concerns about how this work would be assessed and if it would qualify toward tenure and promotion activities (Nicotera et al., 2022). Nevertheless, the Carnegie Classification of Institutions of Higher Education shows many institutions across the nation that have adopted CES.

## Example of Community-Engaged Scholarship

Dr. Samuel Lee, an associate professor of environmental science, is dedicated to community engagement and collaborative solutions to real-world problems. In response to urban heat islands and food deserts, he initiates the Urban Green Initiative (UGI), partnering his university with local government, non-profits, and community groups to promote sustainability through green spaces and community gardens.

Dr. Lee holds meetings with stakeholders, including city planners and residents, to identify areas for green interventions. He then proposes workshops to educate the community on urban gardening and climate resilience. To enhance learning, he integrates UGI into his curriculum, allowing students to facilitate workshops and gain hands-on experience in outreach and project management. They research local biodiversity and contribute to community assessments.

The initiative benefits the community by increasing access to fresh produce and green spaces, while students apply classroom knowledge in real-world contexts. The project leads to several established community gardens that serve as outdoor classrooms. Dr. Lee and his students collect data to evaluate the initiative's impact, enriching his scholarship and informing future program improvements, ensuring ongoing sustainability and engagement.

## Public Scholarship

Scholarly work through Boyer's lens could fit in more than one category. In addition, scholarship informs teaching and, in many cases, can include public outreach. Therefore, public scholarship is a growing practice, which reflects the practice of sharing academic research with audiences outside of the traditional college to address social issues (Bold.org, 2024). Colbeck and Michael (2006) presented an argument for the inclusion of public scholarship as a category for faculty engagement. Yapa (2006) described public scholarship as academic work that plays a role in generating new knowledge through thoughtful consideration of community engagement issues. It integrates research, teaching, and service, recognizing that valuable insights are not simply transferred from the university to the community. Instead, knowledge is cultivated through its real-world application, which strengthens the university's mission in both education and research.

Public scholarship incorporates all aspects of the work of faculty. It includes "systematic inquiry and results in publicly observable community property that is open to critique and available for others to use and develop" (Colbeck & Michael, 2006, p. 7–8). "Individual faculty may conduct academic work in an integrated way, using their research to inform their teaching, their service and teaching as sources of ideas for their research, and their teaching as opportunities to provide service to the community as well as foster student learning" (Colbeck & Michael, 2006, p. 10).

Conducting public scholarship involves "academic work in a way that integrates service/application/engagement with discovery/research and teaching/learning" (Colbeck & Michael, 2006, p. 10–11). Public scholarship is the complete integration of faculty expectations in teaching, research, and service.

### *Example of Public Scholarship*

For several years I (Brenda) was both faculty and a part-time administrator, holding the title of Director of Strategic Partnerships. In this role, I managed field placement adjuncts and two staff members. Together we oversaw the placement of all student teachers. In addition, I also wrote grants to support university-K-12 partnerships. Placing teachers with qualified cooperating teachers became more and more challenging over the years as cooperating teachers became hesitant to give over their students to a new teacher, in light of state testing requirements. It was time to come up with a new plan!

While attending a conference, I learned about a co-teaching model that other universities were implementing with great success with K-12 schools. I attended a train-the-trainer seminar and approached schools with this new model. Overwhelmingly, schools were excited to pilot it. But this also meant I needed to train the co-teaching partners in how to become co-teachers. This was going to take a lot of time, but it had such tremendous potential that I needed to go ahead with it. I enlisted the help of a colleague, who was also interested in this model, and I found a small grant to support a pilot. I launched the pilot with one high school. The grant supported stipends for the cooperating teachers and snacks for the after school professional development. At the end of the semester, the school was committed to taking even more student teachers the following year and the entire district wanted to participate.

The school district had a partnership with my institution and another university. It was important we all worked together. As I met with colleagues from the neighboring university, we talked about the possibility of expanding to additional districts and creating a much larger group. We ended up with multiple school districts, two universities, a training model, and a model for pairing the co-teachers.

To support this work, we wrote two grants, covering multiple years, totaling more than $1 million and I conducted multiple research studies. These studies yielded several publications and national conference presentations, meeting the threshold for public scholarship.

## OTHER SCHOLARLY ACTIVITIES

The scholarship models discussed provide one way forward, but there are many other activities that can contribute to your curriculum vitae and your growth and development as a scholar. We offer two examples: membership in organizations and serving as a peer-reviewer for a journal. First, identify organizations prominent in your discipline and join one. This is a great way to network by joining special interest groups, attending their yearly conference, and even joining collaborative research projects. Organizations with yearly conferences also need volunteers to review proposals. Attending the yearly conference is recommended to stay up-to-date on the latest research in your field and network with those conducting the research.

Early on in my academic career, I (Brenda) attended the American Educational Research Association (AERA) conference. When I registered for the conference, I joined a special interest group, which had a special gathering for junior faculty to meet with senior faculty members for two hours of mentoring. It was an amazing experience!

Volunteering to be a peer-reviewer for a journal is another way to gain valuable experience. The first journal I reviewed for had an acceptance rate of less than 10%. This was a journal I had targeted for my own work, but I was intimidated by the acceptance rate. I read a couple of manuscripts every year and became familiar with the rubric and what the editors were expecting. What I learned shaped my own manuscript.

## SCHOLARSHIP AND PROFESSIONAL ATTAINMENT: THE BASICS

One of the most basic premises of being a scholar is maintaining your subject matter expertise. Fields evolve rapidly, especially in the age of AI. Scholars must engage with new scholarship in their field by reading scholarship material, participating in professional organizations, and attending conferences. Participation in these activities is one level of professional attainment and scholarship. Leadership in these areas is important as well and could be a way to develop as a professional and to serve your discipline.

Research is not only valued at the faculty level—it is a practice we should be teaching our students. As mentioned in Chapters 1 and 2, undergraduate research is a high-impact practice (HIP), and many institutions engage student across all disciplines in research experiences (AACU, 2024). In order to teach or guide research, it is important to become a practicing researcher. Although our terminal degrees included our dissertation work, we stress the importance of maintaining your momentum when you earn that doctorate.

Working toward a first publication or presentation can be intimidating. Dr. Lewis has already completed the hard work of a research study, giving her a great place to start for her first publication or presentation. We recommend she finds a journal that matches her dissertation topic. One way to do this is for Dr. Lewis to review her reference list and make a list of the journals the authors she cited published in. With a short list of journals, she can then go to Cabells (Cabells.com) to find detailed information about each journal. Cabells provides information such as type of review, acceptance rates, time to publication from acceptance, length of manuscripts, and citation style. From there, Dr. Lewis can go to the journal website and learn more about the scope of the journal and tips for authors.

We caution that not all journals have the same goals. Predatory journals are those that offer an open-access model, requiring the author to pay to publish in their journal. These can cost the author thousands of dollars. Predatory journals have been known to publish poor quality research. Cabells supports the researcher by providing information on high-quality journals so you can avoid the predatory journal model.

Many national and state organizations have their own journals. Many conferences also offer presenters with the opportunity to submit papers to be considered for published conference proceedings. By doing a bit of digging, Dr. Lewis can find the right place for her dissertation work.

## BEYOND THE BASICS

Many universities offer faculty development support. We would encourage Dr. Lewis to visit that department to learn what support they can offer her. For example, it is common for workshops on academic writing, research planning, and publishing strategies to be offered to faculty. Attending these could give Dr. Lewis a solid foundation to launch her scholarship. We also encourage new faculty to seek opportunities to serve as a peer-reviewer for high-quality journals. Perhaps you have already joined an organization with prominence in your discipline. Engage with that organization through peer-review of manuscripts submitted to their journal, or peer-review conference proposals. This professional collaboration gives you a behind-the-scenes look at how journals score manuscripts, time from submission to review decision, as well as a good look at what topics the journal publishes. The same is true of conference proposals. These activities not only help you grow as a scholar, but they often also contribute to your service requirements of your institution.

Faculty scholarship is an expectation in higher education. In fact, "academics are expected to create new knowledge and expand the boundaries of the known world" (Sword, 2017, p. 169). We empathize with the stress and anxiety that Dr. Lewis is experiencing knowing she needs help but is afraid to reveal what she does not know. As faculty mentors, we would encourage her to seek out university supports like a faculty development center. If the university offers a new faculty training group, use those meetings to ask specific questions. These groups are designed to field a range of questions and to help 'set up' the new faculty member for success. And, no one expects you to know all of the answers, after all, you are new!

## SELF-MENTORSHIP

We engage in scholarship to deepen our own knowledge and to expand the knowledge within our field. We do so as life-long learners, eager to dig into topics and disciplines we are passionate about. In the Mentoring Moments exercises for this chapter (Exercises 4.1-4.3), you will be challenged to think about your research through multiple models, brainstorm ideas for scholarly activities, and explore support available to you through your university. Set aside intentional time for self-mentorship. By the time you finish this set of activities, you will be more than ready for Chapter 5.

## REFERENCES

AACU. (2024). High impact practices. https://www.aacu.org/trending-topics/high-impact

Berg, M., & Seeber, B. K. (2017). *The slow professor: Challenging the culture of speed in the academy*. University of Toronto Press.

Bold.org. (2024, June 2). The rise of public scholarship. https://bold.org/blog/the-rise-of-public-scholarship/

Boyer, E. L. (1990). *Scholarship reconsidered: Priorities of the professoriate*. Princeton University Press.

Carnegie Classification of Institutions of Higher Education. (n.d.). *Elective classifications: Community engagement*. American Council on Education. Retrieved January 28, 2025, from https://carnegieclassifications.acenet.edu/elective-classifications/community-engagement/ https://carnegieclassifications.acenet.edu/elective-classifications/community-engagement/

Colbeck, C. L., & Michael, P. W. (2006). The public scholarship: Reintegrating Boyer's four domains. *New directions for institutional research*, 2006(129), 7–19. https://doi.org/10.1002/ir.168

Fairweather J.S. (1993). *Teaching, research and faculty rewards: A summary of the research findings of the faculty profile project*. National Center on Postsecondary Teaching, Learning and Assessment, Pennsylvania State University.

Glassick, CE., Huber, MT., Maeroff, G. (1997) Scholarship Assessed. Jossey-Bass.

Hutchings, P., & Shulman, L. S. (1999). The scholarship of teaching: New elaborations, new developments. *Change: The Magazine of Higher learning*, *31*(5), 10–15. https://doi.org/10.1080/00091389909604218

Janke, E., Quan, M., Jenkins, I., Saltmarsh, J., & Janke, E. M. (2023). We're Talking About Process: The Primacy of Relationship and Epistemology in Defining Community-engaged Scholarship in Promotion and Tenure Policy. *Michigan Journal of Community Service Learning*, *29*(1). https://journals.publishing.umich.edu/mjcsl/article/id/2734/

Nibert, M. (2001). *Boyer's model of scholarship*. Pacific Crest Faculty Development Series.

Nicotera, N., Cutforth, N., Fretz, E., & Thompson, S.S. (2022). Dedication to community engagement: A higher education conundrum? *Journal of community engagement and scholarship*, *4*(1). https://compact.org/sites/default/files/2022-06/Dedication%20to%20Community%20Engagement_%20A%20Higher%20Education%20Conundrum_.pdf

O'meara, K., Eatman, T., & Petersen, S. (2015). Advancing engaged scholarship in promotion and tenure: A roadmap and call for reform. *Liberal education*, *101*(3), n3. https://compact.org/sites/default/files/2022-05/Advancing%20Engaged%20Scholarship%20in%20P%26T.pdf

Post, M. A., Ward, E., Longo, N. V., & Saltmarsh, J. (Eds.). (2016). *Publicly engaged scholars: Next-generation engagement and the future of higher education*. Stylus Publishing.

Sword, H. (2017). *Air & light & time & space: How successful academics write*. Harvard University Press.

Yapa, L. (2006). Public scholarship in the postmodern university. *New Directions for Teaching and Learning*, *2006*(105), 73–83. https://doi.org/10.1002/tl.226

# Chapter 5

# Planning and Engaging in Scholarship

## FACULTY FOCUS

*Dr. Ramírez, a new assistant professor in SocialWork, is eager to start her academic career, aiming to contribute research and impact her students positively. However, she quickly encounters challenges in balancing her heavy teaching load, service responsibilities, and research ambitions. Assigned three different courses each semester, Dr. Ramírez spends substantial time preparing lectures and grading, which limits her research time. Additionally, her committee assignments and the department's teaching-focused environment hinder her ability to pursue her research goals. Without a research-driven community or collaborators, she finds it difficult to stay motivated and current in her field. Adjusting to institutional policies, advising students, and building collegial relationships further add to her stress, leaving her discouraged about her stalled research agenda. Despite publishing one paper from her dissertation, Dr. Ramírez struggles to make significant progress on her scholarship, feeling that her academic aspirations are slipping away.*

## INTRODUCTION

Scholarship is often seen as that "thing" that can get moved to the margins. After all, unlike the student standing in our doorway, journals are not waiting at our door for our submission. In Chapter 4, we explored different models of scholarship. We learned that regardless of institution type, whether focused on research or primarily on teaching', scholarship is an expectation. It has become central to the tenure and promotion process (O'Meara et al., 2015). But this isn't the only reason it is important. Engaging in scholarship results in a multitude of benefits. On a personal level, we build to our own academic growth and professional development by expanding our knowledge and expertise. In our teaching, we strengthen our own course content and instruction by including recent research, best practices, and new technological tools. By sharing our work, we also model curiosity and discovery for our students. We contribute to a community of knowledge both inside and outside academia.

DOI: 10.4324/9781003484196-9

The purpose of this chapter is to describe ways to plan for and engage in scholarship. Over the course of the chapter, we confront challenges often faced by faculty and provide suggestions on how to plan for and engage in scholarship. We begin with a discussion of how to identify a topic for your research and how to focus and align your work. Next, we tackle time, writing space, and goal setting. Then we move into a discussion about how to network, find mentorship, collaborate with colleagues, and use conferences as a place to meet other like-minded colleagues. Last, we discuss tools to help support professional attainment and scholarly work.

## PLANNING FOR SCHOLARSHIP

Every institution has their own expectations for scholarly attainment, as do disciplines. Every institution sets unique standards for scholarly achievement. In addition, academic disciplines vary in their methodologies, rigor, and research priorities. Discipline-specific expectations may include requirements for publication or theoretical contributions. We encourage you to read through your faculty handbook, talk with colleagues, and meet with your leadership to ensure you understand the tenure and promotion process, expectations, and support for scholarship. The same goes for your discipline. Years ago, a dear friend of mine asked me to read through an article she was submitting to a top-tier journal. I was very surprised when I opened the document to find it was more than 60 pages in length! I immediately wrote to her and asked a few questions and learned that in her discipline, this type of submission was the norm. In education, however, our articles rarely exceed 35 pages. She did her homework and knew what was expected, which set her up for success. In addition, before she wrote even one word, she had to identify what she would write about.

### Identify a Research Focus

In academia, there is freedom to choose research topics. However, for some professionals this is like walking into your favorite bookstore and being told only to select one book—how do you choose? Several academic coaches recommend creating your academic mission statement. If you wish to be a bit less formal, another option might be to identify your focus by selecting a topic.

During a conversation, a colleague discussed her research using the metaphor of an umbrella. I was intrigued. She described the umbrella as the overarching topic that encompassed the research she had engaged in and where she wanted to go next. It was where all scholarly work fit under one significant topic. Maintaining a focus on topics that fit under the umbrella enables researchers to build knowledge and expertise in a specific field of knowledge. Therefore, we recommend you identify the area(s) you wish to focus your work. Then, determine what you want to come from your work. For example, some scholars/professors use their research and academic voice for social advocacy, while others share creative works or breakthrough medical research. Whatever your goal or mission, identify it in a way that makes your research concrete and attainable. Cathy Mazak offers advice on how to write an academic mission statement on her website. You can find this at https://scholarsvoice.org/academic-mission-statement/. Mazak encourages academics to revisit their mission statement at the beginning of each semester and during the summer to see if edits are needed.

One of my doctoral students commented on how she was surprised I (Brenda) was still writing on the same topic as my dissertation all these years later. Over time, my topic or umbrella has expanded to a more inclusive topic, but the focus has not changed. This affords me the ability to be strategic in how I respond to invitations. If the activity aligns with my academic mission, I can say yes. If, however, it is outside my academic mission, I then take time to determine if this activity or project is a good fit.

## Where to Begin

With your academic mission established, it is time to dive in! For many in academia, their dissertation represents a topic they are passionate about. This was true for me (Brenda), and as soon as I had defended my dissertation, it was time to pursue publishing my work. This would be my first time submitting a manuscript to a peer-reviewed journal, and I was not completely sure where to start. I decided to look at my reference list. I was citing these journals, after all, so perhaps my work would fit in one of these publications. I found a handful of journals that I regularly cited in my work. I then looked up each journal to learn about the submission requirements, including the scope and sequence of the discipline, format requirements, length, review timeline, and acceptance percentages. From there, I chose one journal for my first attempt at academic publishing. I then spent time reading articles found in the most recent issue. After selecting three research articles from that issue, I created a journal template. To create the template, I took the average number of words in each section from the recent articles and calculated the average number of references. I added this information to each section heading to provide a guide as I began to work. Creating a template offered a couple of benefits. First, I appreciated the template as a guide. Second, and perhaps more importantly, I had a document with words and an outline. It felt like I had already begun writing because the page was no longer blank! Years later, I continue this practice and have shared this tip with colleagues, who have also found this practice helpful.

If you have published your dissertation, do you still have interest in the topic? If so, we encourage you to identify the next article. Perhaps re-read your chapter five. What recommendations did you get for future research on your topic? Are these recommendations still relevant? If you have decided to go in a new direction, use Google Scholar to determine whether or not the topic is an emerging trend or fills a research gap. Begin reading and creating a literature review. Are there gaps in the field that you wish to explore? Can you identify key questions or problems to address? Once you have these answers, you are ready to engage in scholarship.

## ENGAGING IN SCHOLARSHIP

We are often asked by colleagues how we are able to publish consistently. This is often followed up with the colleague explaining how busy they are and how taxing their teaching load is, leaving no time for scholarship. We can relate!

### Time

Several authors we enjoy have written on the concept of time and finding time to write. Mazak (2022) wrote, "The great irony of academic culture is that while publications are revered, writing time is relegated to the periphery of our calendars" (p. 74). As faculty members, we don't give a second thought to adding meetings, committee tasks, and student meetings on our calendar; yet we hesitate to designate time for scholarship. Teaching is scheduled and your writing time should be, too (Silvia, 2014).

A colleague commented that she felt guilty for designating time to writing because it was taking away from her ability to meet with students. To be clear, we are not advocating that faculty neglect their students. On the contrary, we are reminding you that as faculty, engaging in scholarship is a requirement of our job. Faculty are evaluated on their teaching, service, and scholarship. Therefore, we must prioritize time to engage in all three activities.

How do we find time? In reading Sword (2017), I laughed out loud (Brenda) when she said, "You can't lose time behind the back of a sofa or discover a forgotten stash tucked away in a kitchen drawer" (p. 17). Time is not found; it is managed and protected. Silvia (2014) encourages academics to "ruthlessly defend your writing time" (p. 15). You have a job to do. Set firm boundaries and stick to them. It took a bit of time for this advice/wisdom to sink in.

I struggled at the beginning of my career to wrangle time. I tried keeping track of where my time went. I attempted to schedule each day and, at the end of the day, account for my hours. I was intentional about turning down requests for my time in many instances; yet, I could not get any momentum in my writing. I needed something different. I needed something consistent. The answer came with my own scheduling. Before the beginning of each semester, I grab a cup of coffee and sit down with my calendar. I chart out my classes and office hours. I then mark myself out for conferences, even if I have yet to submit a proposal.

Next, I add committee dates, and department meetings, if known. Then I look at my calendar for chunks of time. Silvia (2014) says the key is regularity, not the number of hours each week. Perhaps for you, writing time consists of a couple of hours each Wednesday, a half-day every Tuesday, or one hour twice a week. Whatever it is, grab that time now and mark yourself "out" for scholarship. Then, commit to protecting this time by considering it a nonnegotiable part of your day. This time is as important as your office hours or teaching—your university told you so with how you are evaluated.

## Physical Space

With your time protected, determine where you will spend that time. Writing is portable, which means that you are not confined to one space. Can you work in your office, or will you be interrupted? Where do you feel the most comfortable? Take a look at your university campus. Do you have a library where you can reserve a small space, or is there a quiet spot you can use consistently? Or is a coffee shop better for you? Perhaps white noise and a hot coffee are what you need! I love my local library and local coffee shops. They are close to home and provide a space where I can spread out my books and journal articles and still have room for my laptop. Our university library is also a great writing choice. I found comfortable chairs with a table overlooking the quad. It is tucked away, and as far as I have seen, few people use this spot. I also find that leaving my office is a physical way to keep the appointments I have with myself without getting distracted by the papers on my desk.

## Goal Setting and Research Schedule

As educators, we both promote backward design, a method developed by Grant Wiggins and Jay McTighe (2005) as a way to design curriculum. The basic idea is to start with the end in mind. This process has great applications to writing. As mentioned previously, determine a topic and then decide on a journal. From there, I create a template from prior published articles so that my manuscript is in the correct format. A quick look at the journal website will reveal any deadlines for submission. With this knowledge, you are now able to work backwards.

Determining when and how often to write can be challenging. For example, setting a goal to write every day can backfire. Things happen and before you know it, you were only able to write two out of the five days. Now, to be clear, this is a win! You wrote twice in one week! However, if not meeting the goal to write every day makes you feel like you have failed, it is time to set a different goal. Perhaps writing one to two hours once or twice a week is the perfect plan for you, or writing four hours in one day works best. Whatever it is, set a goal and protect that time.

For each writing session, set a realistic goal. For example, you may be working on writing a new article. Perhaps your goal is to create the template based on the journal you selected, or maybe you have the template and wish to write 200 words for the introduction. It may be that you wish to submit a conference proposal and need to write a short literature review. Whatever it is, write a concise and measurable goal. For support, we recommend the workbook *Writing Your Journal Article in Twelve Weeks: A Guide to Academic Publishing Success* by Wendy Belcher. The book is fantastic for setting goals, working through the writing process step-by-step, and evaluating your work prior to submission. At the end of each writing session, take a moment to make yourself notes on where you left off. This way you will not lose time during your next writing session trying to figure out what your next step was meant to be. Another strategy is to track your progress through each writing session. One of my dear friends has a spreadsheet where she tracks each writing session by recording her word count. At the end of each writing session, she is able to see her accomplishment. By tracking your progress, you can see your article grow and you can celebrate your progress. This keeps you accountable and on track. For my friend, her system also helped her to see what days and times she was the most productive, leading to her moving her writing times to maximize when she is most successful. Whatever system you use and whatever goals you set, we encourage you to celebrate when you meet your goal or hit a milestone.

## What "Counts" as Writing?

When I read Silvia's (2014) book, *Write It Up: Practical Strategies for Writing and Publishing Journal Articles,* I was excited to see that "writing" is not just "writing" but includes a number of activities that lead up to you adding words on a page. He defines writing as any activity that assists the writing project. This includes: searching for articles, reading articles, analyzing data, searching for the right journal for your own submission, creating the template for your article, creating tables or figures from your data, and the list continues. Create your goals with these activities in mind and celebrate when you successfully meet your goal of finding five peer-reviewed articles during your writing session. I find that Silva's definition has contributed to a positive frame of mind when I am working on a deadline. Every writing session can be successful, but they look different based on targeted goals for my writing engagement.

## Writing Tools

There is a plethora of writing tools, both free and paid. In addition, artificial intelligence (AI) tools continue to grow at a rapid pace. We share a handful of tools we have used in Table 5.1 Writing Tools, and then engage in a conversation around the ethical use of AI.

*Table 5.1* Writing Tools

| Tool | Notes | Link |
|---|---|---|
| Academic Phrasebank | This resource was created by Dr. Morley from Manchester University. It is available in three formats; an interactive PDF, Kindle, and as a paperback. The resource contains thousands of commonly used phrases in academic writing to help academic writers diversify their sentences. | https://www.phrasebank.manchester.ac.uk/ |
| The Pomodoro Technique | This method uses a timer to break work into short intervals with short breaks. For example, if you have a two-hour writing block, you could break your time into 25-minute work sessions, along with a five-minute break, then another 25-minute work session, etc. By limiting time, it creates a sense of urgency, which encourages the user to stop procrastinating and get down to business. For those who wish to build time in to read texts or emails, setting the timer gives focused time, followed by a short break to respond when needed. | https://www.pomodorotechnique.com/ |
| Inbox Pause | A way to stop emails from coming in until you are finished with your writing session. If you are someone who is distracted by seeing or hearing emails arrive in your inbox, this could be a tool for you. | https://inboxpause.com/ |
| Toggl | A time-tracking app you can add to your phone or computer. It can help you determine how long it takes for you to complete a task, which could help you adjust your writing blocks as needed. | https://toggl.com/ |
| Forest | A creative way to encourage focused work time. If you tend to pick up your phone when you should be writing, this app could help you. You set the time you wish for your focused time. During that period of time, you will grow a tree. If, however, you pick up your phone to go out of the app, the tree dies. Successful focused time, over multiple sessions, results in a forest. It works like a focused time management game. | https://www.forestapp.cc/ |

*(Continued)*

*Table 5.1* (Continued)

| Tool | Notes | Link |
|---|---|---|
| Trello | A project management program where you can create a "board" for each writing project. You can use this to create your roadmap for multiple articles or research projects. You can create lists called "cards", which you can move. You can add due dates, files, lists, links, etc. This is a great brainstorming tool as well. You can also use it to collaborate with co-authors. | https://trello.com |
| Zotero | A management system for journal articles. It is free and easy to use and a great way to organize your articles into writing projects, save references from your browser, and create bibliographies. Users love the ability to cite as they write using Zotero. | https://www.zotero.org/ |
| Grammarly | Grammarly is an AI writing tool that provides suggestions for the author on grammar, spelling, punctuation, style, and tone. Before you begin writing, you can choose various settings to help Grammarly understand the audience for your work. | https://grammarly.com |

In addition to the tools we have mentioned, AI is an important tool that cannot be ignored. When using AI, there are several important considerations to keep in mind. First, you need to be aware of the difference between AI-assisted and AI-generated. Using tools to assist or strengthen your writing is accepted by most peer-reviewed journals. AI-generated texts, however, are not acceptable. Asking ChatGPT to assist by formatting your references in a specific citation style is seen as AI-assisted. Asking ChatGPT to create a reference list on a specific topic is AI-generated. We have seen journals asking authors whether or not their work has been AI-generated and requiring an answer before submission of the manuscript. Next, AI is known to hallucinate. This means AI can create things that look real but do not exist. For example, a graduate student asked AI to identify dissertations on a specific topic with a narrow focus. AI came back with three. However, when she went to locate these, the student found that all three had been made up by the AI program.

## The Peer-Review Process

Peer-reviewed journals ensure vetted and quality research by experts in the field, which adds credibility to academic work. These journals also prioritize original contributions with significant findings in order to advance disciplinary knowledge. The peer-review process takes time, and it may be 4–6 months after an author submit a manuscript before a decision is made. More often than not, the journal will accept, accept with minor revisions, or request that you revise and resubmit. The decision will come with reviewer comments, which can be helpful. I say "can" be helpful because sometimes reviews come with conflicting advice. For example, one reviewer commented that my theoretical framework was well done and connected well with my study. Reviewer 2, however, said my theoretical framework needed significant work due to misalignment with my research project. Reviewer 3 made no comment about my theoretical framework. Now, if you need a good laugh, you can find many memes and even social media sites dedicated entirely to Reviewer 2, but that does not make it any easier to know how to respond. Both of us have been in this situation more than once. One way to move forward is to create a table with all of the comments you received, organized by reviewer number. In the next column you provide your response to the comment made. It is important to note that reviewer comments are not prescriptive. If you disagree with a comment, you can explain your rationale for not making a change so that the editor can follow you train of thought. Recently, a reviewer suggested it was necessary for a political statement to be made in the manuscript. My co-author and I disagreed, as we felt it was inappropriate for our research article. I included a statement in my table explaining why that comment was disregarded. The article was published without any further discussion. In other words, it is okay to disagree with other experts in the field—you will be an expert with your own opinions and voice.

## CREATING YOUR SCHOLARLY IDENTITY

Academia offers many opportunities to engage activities. It can be a bit challenging to navigate that new road on your own. We recommend finding a mentor, collaborating with colleagues, and engaging in a scholarly community.

### Finding a Mentor

Academia can be isolating if you let it. Everyone is busy and it can be easy to assume a closed office door also means that the colleague is closed to connection. We encourage you to reach out to your colleagues, find a mentor, seek opportunities to collaborate, and consider creating a writing group. You might be surprised by who joins you!

My first year in academia, I (Brenda) was blessed to have a colleague take me under their wing. It began with a colleague simply inviting me to coffee. The first few months, she asked how I was settling in, how my classes were going, whether I was finding a rhythm to my new position. I remember leaving our coffee appointments feeling relieved and reassured that I was on the right path. Every year she would review my Curriculum Vitae, talk through conferences she thought could be a good fit for me, and even offered to review conference proposals. As a full tenured professor, she had a lot of wisdom to share and I was eager to learn from her. We became good friends. Just last week she sent me a message to congratulate me on an accomplishment. Her words of encouragement and wisdom are invaluable.

We encourage you to find a mentor. Who in your department is researching and publishing? Is there anyone writing and researching on your topic or area of interest? Anyone in your department good at grant writing? Is there a skill you want to learn? We are never too new or too far into our career to seek the help of others. Take a few minutes to consider the mentorship you are looking for, find people with those skills, and invite them to coffee.

## Collaborating with Colleagues

As you begin to engage in scholarly activities, will you write alone or find a colleague for support and accountability? Writing alone and in community has both benefits and drawbacks. I (Jodi) began my writing as a doctoral student. I had an amazing professor at Texas Woman's University, Dr. Betty Carter, who encouraged me to publish some action research I'd conducted for her class. I had no idea what I was doing, but she guided me through the process, and I was thrilled to see my article in print! I had caught the writing bug, but it would be many years later before I published my next scholarly article. The topic would be dyslexia, as this disability had affected my children, and I wanted to share what I had learned about it through research and experience with others. Research often starts with passion about a topic.

As social media became a hot topic in the early 2000s, I was fascinated by how technology could be leveraged by teachers to motivate and engage K-12 students. I have built my research agenda around digital literacies for almost twenty years now, but I was intentional in finding other colleagues with similar interests. I have found that by writing with colleagues, you expand your knowledge base, learn from one another and gain momentum by brainstorming ideas. I have learned a great deal from my co-author Sheri Vasinda. Sheri and I both served on the board of the Texas Association of Literacy Education. I was impressed with her work ethic and began seeing her at state, national, and international literacy conferences. After attending her presentation on the instructional use of iPads, I approached her about working together on an iPad project. By the end of the year, we had published our first article together, along with two other colleagues. We quickly learned we not only had similar interests and research agendas; we also had a similar work ethic. Writing with others can be frustrating, so I cannot stress the importance of work ethic enough. There will be instances where your writing time occurs during your personal time. For me, there was no way around it.

I was unable to teach, advise, serve, and write during the workday. If I was going to extend extra effort on publication, I expected others to do so as well. Sheri and I were both equally committed to our deadlines, even if it meant late nights. Sheri is in Oklahoma (OSU) and I'm in Texas, so this has meant many working Zoom/Teams sessions. During some research projects, it was essential we scheduled weekly meetings to maintain our momentum for enhanced productivity. We utilized other technology tools like Google Docs, Microsoft OneDrive, and Dropbox for our co-writing endeavors. Sheri and I present on one of our projects every year, which requires a lot of advanced planning. For example, proposals for national conferences are typically due almost a year before the next conference.

Sheri and I share a mutual respect for each other and are both encouraging and motivating. Recently, after reading "Reviewer 2's" comments, Sheri, as the primary author on the piece, was ready to throw in the towel on a peer-reviewed book chapter. We had already engaged in the project for a year, and I was not ready to see that work go unpublished. I reworked the chapter and sent it to Sheri for one last attempt at the resubmission process. Even though the reworked chapter needed a lot more work from Sheri, seeing the work from a different angle was the motivation she needed to move forward. I am pleased to share that the chapter on the TPACK framework was accepted for publication in the upcoming 3rd edition of the *Handbook of Technological Pedagogical Content Knowledge (TPACK) for Educators*.

## Creating a Writing Group

A couple of years ago, I (Brenda) moved from Oregon to Texas to join the College of Education at the University of Mary Hardin-Baylor. I left behind a writing group I began six years earlier. I wanted an opportunity to get to know my colleagues and I also wanted a writing accountability and support group. I launched a writing group for our college that fall. I modeled our group after the one I founded at my previous institution. In our first session, we shared our goals and reasons for joining the group. We then identified professional development that would help us move our work forward. I then invited others to come and offer us training during our writing session. For example, our group wanted to learn how to use Zotero. The librarian who was designated to the College of Education was more than happy to come and provide this training. She was actually so excited about our group that she asked if she could join us.

During our first year together, we each purchased the book *Writing Your Journal Article in Twelve Weeks: A Guide to Academic Publishing Success* by Belcher (2019). We divided the chapters by our academic year and discussed the chapters at each writing session. We all committed to submitting an article, or conference proposal by the end of the academic year.

Each 60-minute writing session, every other week, begins by sharing our writing goals, asking for help when needed, and assisting others when requested. We also share our successes and breakthroughs. This usually takes about 10–15 minutes. We then write for about 40–45 minutes. We spend the last few minutes sharing how the session went for us and if we could use help or support before our next session. By the end of the academic year, the majority of members met their goal of submitting a manuscript.

The writing group is in its' fourth year and going strong! Since the first year, we extended our meeting time from 60 to 90 minutes. We also read the book *Write It Up* by Paul Silva (2014). The book is an easy read, as Silva has a wonderful sense of humor and excellent writing tips. Our group also expanded to include friends from other colleges, graduate students in our college, and an associate provost. The more time we spend together, the more we can share scholarship opportunities with each other as we know what we are all researching and writing about.

Our group has been successful. I attribute this to the trust we have built within our group. We created a safe space where everyone can ask questions they may have been afraid to ask, believing they may be judged for not knowing the answer. We have also fostered cross-disciplinary collaboration and conversation, yielding personal and professional growth. The structure, support, and accountability of this group have produced results. Since launching this group, all of our members have had conference proposals accepted and manuscripts published. Our experience is an example of what Mazak (2022) calls the "community over accountability" (p. 100). She explains how we can often confuse accountability with what we really need; community. There is power when a group comes together to support and celebrate with one another.

## Finding a Scholarly Community

One of our university colleagues successfully defended her dissertation a little over a year ago. New to academia, and with her fresh off the press dissertation, she knew it was time to publish and present her work. She was unfamiliar with organizations and conferences within her discipline that could be a good fit. She wrote to a few faculty in her department and asked what conferences they were presenting at and what organizations they were members of. She then took this information and evaluated each organization and conference through the lens of her research to see where she might fit. She was excited when her first conference proposal was accepted and grateful to her colleagues for their support. Her discipline is business and she found her "people" quickly. My (Brenda) journey has included a number of twists and turns. I am in education, but I specialize in trauma-response, a topic more common in social work and mental health circles. Some of the conferences of these disciplines are only open to faculty with those degrees, so it has taken me some time to find my people. At one point I wrote to several authors of articles I cited regularly to ask what conferences they attended.

They were gracious and responded with names and recommendations. We encourage you to follow the example of our business colleague. Talk with the faculty in your hallway to find out more about what conferences they are attending and presenting at. Many organizations also have special interest groups, which provide smaller groups for people with a particular interest in one segment of a larger topic. This is a great way to network and collaborate across multiple states and campuses. Research Gate, Google Scholar, LinkedIn, and other social media and academic platforms are also a great place to meet other like-minded people and stay up-to-date on trends in your field. In addition to membership in professional organizations and conference attendance, there are many other ways to engage in a scholarly community. One we wish to draw your attention to is Fulbright.

## Fulbright

A colleague received a Fulbright Scholar award to teach in Austria for a year. I (Brenda) was intrigued; this sounded like an adult study abroad with amazing financial support! Fulbright was founded in 1946. The goal of Fulbright is to create opportunities for people from the United States to collaborate with people from other countries. This is accomplished by offering extensive scholarships and fellowships in more than 160 countries (https://fulbrightprogram.org/about/). Deadlines, timelines, funding, and eligibility vary depending on the fellowship or scholarship.

When my colleague returned, she offered a professional development workshop on Fulbright awards, shared her application, and offered to help others with an application. I was a few years away from being eligible for sabbatical, but I attended her workshop and took copious notes. For the next couple of years, whenever my husband and I traveled internationally, we would ask ourselves: "Is this a place we would be interested in living for a year?"

When the time came to apply for sabbatical, I submitted a Fulbright Scholar application to teach and research in Estonia. It was a big day in our home when I got the news that I was chosen! My experience in Estonia and with Fulbright turned out to be life-changing. Not only did I have an unbelievable experience, I was able to create relationships with two of the largest universities in Estonia, resulting in a faculty position at one institution, collaborative grant activities, research, and trainings. I have traveled to Estonia more than 10 times in the last six years and am in my fifth year as a Visiting Professor at Tallinn University.

Before I left Estonia at the end of my Scholar award, I was encouraged to apply to the Fulbright Specialist roster. The Fulbright Scholar program offers awards to 160 countries. I took this encouragement, was accepted and placed on the roster, and had a funded project for 2022. The project was to provide trauma-response training to teachers and social workers in three regions of Estonia with three university partners. While the trip was planned more than nine months in advance, the timing resulted in me landing in Estonia four days after Russia invaded Ukraine. When I arrived, thousands of Ukrainian refugee women and children had also arrived in Estonia. I spent five weeks training teachers and helping leaders prepare and respond to traumatized people.

I cannot recommend Fulbright programs highly enough. They are a competitive fellowship that is prestigious and can assist with your tenure and promotion. As they tout on their website, Fulbright programs create connections and cultivate collaboration (Fulbright.org). Many Fulbright Scholars go on to teach, research, and publish with their host country colleagues. In fact, a study exploring publication activity of alumni found that after their award, co-publication with the host institution increased from 16% to 51% (https://fulbrightscholars.org/who-we-are/why-fulbright-stands-apart). In addition, membership in this community provides opportunities for collaboration, service to others heading to the country you just left, and lifelong friendships.

Last week I was in a meeting in which a colleague from the Business Department was talking about wanting to take students to another country for a study abroad. He wanted to make this not just a one-time experience, but was seeking to create a partnership with a university in the country of interest. Another colleague at the table suggested he consider submitting an application to the Fulbright Specialist program. Two of us in the meeting were recipients of this program and immediately offered our own experiences and how this could be a great way to move forward. The three of us made plans to meet the following week to assist with his application. We encourage you to consider Fulbright programs.

## THE BASICS

At the beginning of this chapter, we met Dr. Ramirez, a new assistant professor. In light of the information presented in this chapter, we can see how she would benefit by finding people at her university who are researching and publishing regularly. She could use support. One way to do this is to seek support from university departments, such as faculty development departments, point persons, or people responsible for faculty development. Additionally, they may be able to provide information on trainings, workshops, or seminars to support new scholars. They would be able to recommend people for Dr. Ramirez to connect with who are engaged in scholarship. They could also recommend a mentor, who could help her understand the expectations for scholarship, provide insights into publishing, conference presentations, and guidance on setting realistic goals for her research output.

It would be helpful to Dr. Ramirez if she set small, achievable goals, like preparing her dissertation for publication in a journal or presenting at a regional conference. Small achievements may build her confidence and create momentum for further scholarship. She may also benefit from seeking research collaborations, either within her department or with colleagues from other institutions. This could ease her isolation and provide her with support in navigating the research process. It may take her a semester or two in order for her to find her footing, but recommendations in this chapter will help her launch her scholarship journey.

## BEYOND THE BASICS

As faculty begin to find success researching and publishing, it is a good time for self-assessment. We recommend seeking feedback from respected peers, revising your research agenda regularly to adjust to new insights or opportunities, and reviewing your academic mission statement. This is also a good time to diversity your scholarship output. By this we mean consider publishing in a variety of formats: books, journal articles, chapters, creative works, or writing for public policy. Have you considered engaging with public scholarship and outreach efforts? What about writing for public policy or op-eds? This is a great way to make your research accessible to the public and to advocate for change.

## SELF-MENTORSHIP

Dr. Ramirez is trying to get her feet underneath her, but has faced several challenges. As faculty mentors we would recommend a good self-mentoring goal setting session. This could include writing out the goals she has, the research she would like to undertake, and the barriers she sees to moving forward. Given that her department has a teaching focus we would encourage her to look at faculty bios from other departments at her institution. Read through their CVs. Who is publishing? Who is writing grants? Then, send an email to a couple of them and ask to meet for coffee. Find out how they are engaging in scholarship. Dr. Ramirez needs to find her people, those with similar goals and aspirations, and meet them regularly.

In the Mentoring Moments we provide you with multiple self-mentoring activities. We begin with a self-assessment, followed by the creation of an academic mission statement, goal setting, creating a semester plan, and, last, suggestions for how to create a writing group. This is a large undertaking and will require time and honesty with yourself. It will not do you any good to set unachievable goals. Be realistic. Create boundaries around your time. Celebrate your progress.

## REFERENCES

Belcher, W. L. (2019). *Writing your journal article in twelve weeks: A guide to academic publishing success.* University of Chicago Press.

Mazak, C. (2022). *Making time to write: How to resist the patriarchy and take control of your academic career through writing.* Morgan James Publishing.

O'Meara, K., Eatman, T., & Petersen, S. (2015). Advancing engaged scholarship in promotion and tenure: A roadmap and call for reform. *Liberal education, 101*(3), n3. https://compact.org/sites/default/files/2022-05/Advancing%20Engaged%20Scholarship%20in%20P%26T.pdf

Silvia, P. J. (2014). *Write it up: Practical strategies for writing and publishing journal articles.* American Psychological Association.

Sword, H. (2017). *Air & light & time & space: How successful academics write.* Harvard University Press.

Wiggins, G., & McTighe, J. (2005). *Understanding by design* (Expanded 2nd ed.). Alexandria, VA: Association for Supervision and Curriculum Development.

Chapter 6

# Tracking and Evaluating Scholarship

## FACULTY FOCUS

Dr. Williams has just started her position as an Assistant Professor in the Department of Sociology at a mid-sized university. With a Ph.D. in Sociology and years of experience as a graduate student, she is passionate about her research in social inequality. However, as she transitions into academia, she is feeling overwhelmed by the expectations for tracking and evaluating her scholarly work.

During her first faculty orientation, there was a brief mention of tracking scholarly contributions for tenure, annual reviews, and funding applications, but the specifics were unclear. She is aware that publishing is necessary, but how will her publications be evaluated? Is it just the quantity of manuscripts required for tenure? Does impact factor matter? And how does she keep track of all the papers, citations, and funding applications she will eventually need to report?

## INTRODUCTION

Some sources claim that Albert Einstein once stated, "If we knew what we were doing, it wouldn't be called research." We find this quote both comical and somewhat revealing. While most new faculty will have a foundational understanding of research methods based on graduate work, not all new faculty, like Dr. Williams, will be equipped to independently lead advanced projects right away. Many faculty members must learn how to initiate and develop a research agenda (Brent & Felder, 2016). In other words, they may not know what they are doing yet! Researching takes time.

In Chapter 4, we presented several widely accepted forms of scholarship. In Chapter 5, we discussed how to plan and engage in scholarship. This chapter extends these conversations and provides a structured approach to tracking and evaluating your academic scholarship. We approach this work by suggesting a multi-pronged approach:

1. determine scholarship criteria which will be evaluated at your university,
2. evaluate your productivity through the lens of quality versus quantity,
3. track your progress, self-assess and solicit feedback from peers.

## SCHOLARSHIP CRITERIA

Boyer (1990) and Glassick et al. (1997) provided the foundation for conversations in the field of scholarship, and while many universities have espoused these models, the ways in which faculty are asked to document their work can show an adherence to original models of teaching, research, and service. Therefore, it is imperative you gain understanding of the expectations of your institution.

Faculty tend to spend time on tasks and activities they believe their university values most. Engaging in and documenting scholarship outside the university norm can be detrimental. Therefore, it is imperative that faculty are keenly aware of the expectations and evaluative processes and measures. Once you have clear expectations, you can begin to track and evaluate your scholarship.

Boyer's expanded model of scholarship created new pathways for faculty to engage in scholarly activities. Even though our university uses this model for internal grant applications, our annual faculty evaluation provides a more objective way to measure scholarship or professional attainment. The evaluation instrument clearly presents the scholarship requirements for each level of proficiency, ranging from *does not meet expectations* to *meets expectations* to *exceeds expectations*. During our first year at UMHB, we familiarized ourselves with the annual faculty evaluation to make sure we were on track to meet the required standards. Admittedly, we don't like to simply "meet" expectations, we became familiar with ways to "exceed" expectations. Our evaluation instrument includes criteria for both, so our first step was to understand the standards. We work at a teaching institution, not a research institution, so our scholarship expectations are not as rigorous as those of some other universities.

In tracking and evaluating scholarship, many universities break down criteria to the artifacts we produce. For example, scholarship might result in a presentation, a publication, grant funding, an exhibition, or a performance. The product and level of scholarship attainment is then broken down further for evaluation purposes. Was the presentation a poster presentation? Was it presented at a local or national venue? Was the publication peer-reviewed? If so, what was the journal's impact factor? In the next section, we break down types of scholarship more clearly to address ways to track and rate the level of scholarship produced.

## EVALUATING SCHOLARLY PRODUCTIONS

The evaluation of scholarly works, like presentations and publications, includes several factors. The quantity of research is reflected in the number of publications and presentations, while the quality of scholarly work is reflected in the disciplinary or societal impact the work makes. Lie et al. (2024) suggest that "Excessive attention has been paid to the quantity of research, with scientific institutions emphasizing metrics such as h-index, impact factors of journals, and the number of publications" (para. 1). In this section, we address a few examples of products of scholarship along with considerations of quantity and quality of the work.

## Presentations

Scholarly and creative accomplishments may include peer-reviewed presentations or performances. Presenting at a conference, for example, typically requires a presentation proposal and its acceptance. Conference presentations are an expectation in higher education, as it is one practical method of disseminating your work publicly. The nature of a presentation may vary. Conference presentation categories include poster presentations, roundtable presentations, paper presentations, workshops, panel presentations, and more.

### Quantity vs. Quality

It is possible to fill your Curriculum Vitae (CV) with multiple presentations each year. However, consider the quality of the conference as you evaluate your scholarly achievements. First of all, the peer-review process is more rigorous for some national and international conferences. In the literacy realm, an acceptance to present at the Literacy Research Association conference is far more prestigious than an acceptance by the Texas Association of Literacy Education (TALE). TALE is a state organization, whereas LRA has achieved international recognition.

The type of presentation matters as well. For instance, acceptance of paper presentations for LRA is more of a challenge than roundtable presentations, due to the level of research rigor required in the proposal process. Know your discipline and set goals for your research agenda. Plan ahead because many prestigious conferences start the proposal process for annual conferences 8–12 months before the event date.

## Publications

Scholarly and creative accomplishments may include peer-reviewed publications or compositions. Peer-review is the process your work (manuscript, conference proposal, conference preceding, etc.) goes through to determine journal or organizational fit, quality, rigor, and often impact on the field. Once you have submitted your work, you wait to receive a decision by the editor or committee chair, often accompanied by the peer-review comments of the experts in the field who evaluated your work. The decision could be to accept the manuscript as is, accept with minor revisions, request for a revision and resubmission, or a rejection. It can be frustrating and try your patience as you wait for a decision, but it is the traditional forum for our scholarship to be reviewed and shared.

### Quantity vs. Quality

Metrics such as h-index, impact factors of journals, and the number of publications determine the impact of scholarly publications. The impact factor indicates the quality and popularity of a journal and is defined by the median number of citations for a given period of the articles published in a journal (Lie et al., 2024). An h-index evaluates a researcher's productivity using metrics that determine the number of their manuscripts highly cited within their field (Sahel, 2012). If you are wondering about your colleagues' h-index, check their ResearchGate profile. Platforms like Google Scholar reveal how many times an article has been cited.

A simple way to analyze the quality of a paper may be to look at the reach of the journal. State journals have less viewership than international journals. Some journals that are predatory should be avoided. According to Elmore and Weston (2020), "Predatory journals—also called fraudulent, deceptive, or pseudo-journals—are publications that claim to be legitimate scholarly journals but misrepresent their publishing practices" (para. 1). When we review applicants for faculty positions, we consider the quality and reputation of the journals.

## Grants

Grant writing is a form of scholarship in higher education, in which a faculty member articulates a case for supporting a research project through monetary funding. Funding decisions also include peer-review processes. Many universities offer opportunities for internal grant funding. External grants may include small, local funding opportunities as well as significant funding opportunities from organizations like the National Science Foundation (NSF) or the National Institutes of Health (NIH).

### Quantity vs. Quality

Awards for NSF or NIH grants reflect quality research, as expectations for those grants are high. Success in grant writing is typically equated with the amount of money awarded. Grant awards benefit both the faculty member and the university. Faculty who earn prestigious grants are likely on track for tenure and promotion. However, it is critical that scholarship products come out of the grant work.

## THE BASICS: TRACK YOUR ACTIVITIES

A colleague stopped by my office the other day. He wanted to get some feedback on an idea he had for a chapter proposal. He was excited about the opportunity and said that writing a book chapter would check a box. He is a tenure-track faculty member who will submit his portfolio next year for tenure and promotion consideration. His intentionality with his own scholarship activities was impressive. He knew where he had been and where he needed to venture into. He had a system for tracking his scholarship.

When I started in academia, I was exactly where Dr. Williams is. Just as it is easy to get busy and realize you have not prioritized your scholarship, it is also easy to get into a routine and find that your scholarly activity does not demonstrate a range of activities. A colleague shared his view that after you have published three or four articles on a specific topic, it is time to write a book on that topic. His rationale is that three or four articles indicate you know that topic very well and have likely been engaged with it for years. The point is that you need to keep track of your activities and reflect on where you have been and where to go next.

## Literal Tracking

Tracking does not just mean keeping a mental note. *Literally* track all scholarly activities. Documentation of scholarship can be informal or formal. An informal method may be to start a digital record of accomplishments that you add to consistently. We recommend you add everything from participation in a peer-review process to work on a dissertation committee. Not only do the lists and notes you keep during this process provide a basis for narratives you might include in your tenure and promotion portfolio, they can also demonstrate your efficiency. And, it is satisfying to look back on a year's worth of work to recall the contributions to your discipline and university!

A more formal tracking routine would be to add scholarship accomplishments to your Curriculum Vitae (CV). If you maintain an up-to-date CV, then your record of attainment is ready to share. Tracking may also include the use of social platforms for researchers like Google Scholar, ResearchGate, and Academia. These platforms enable scholars to curate, share, and track their work and its impact. In addition, notifications that someone has downloaded or cited your work can be rewarding.

## BEYOND THE BASICS: SELF-ASSESSMENT AND PEER FEEDBACK

In Chapters 4 and 5, we explored Boyer's (1990) expanded model of scholarship, including discovery, integration, application, and teaching. We also presented ways to participate in public and collaborative scholarship. These models have garnered a plethora of articles and books on how to engage with them, but literature related to the next steps in the process, evaluating your work, is limited. How can faculty evaluate their research?

## Self-Assessment

Self-assessment is one method of evaluating your work in the areas of discovery, integration, application and teaching. Glassick et al. (1997) created a tool by which the Boyer (1990) model could be evaluated. The tool allows for peer-review, in many forms. However, we share the tool as a way to self-assess research standards. Informed by a survey conducted by Carnegie scholars in 1994 (Glassick, 2000), the tool includes a narrative to guide the evaluation of all four categories of scholarship. They concluded that in order for work in the four categories (discovery, integration, application, and teaching) to be considered scholarship, it must include: 1. clear and articulated goals, 2. familiarity of the literature and appropriate skills, 3. appropriate methods, 4. contributions to the field, 5. shared results, 6. critical review of the work. The informational chart in Figure 6.1 shares the accompanying narrative in each category.

The assessment in Figure 6.1 reflects a qualitative assessment of scholarly work. Self-assessment can also include quantitative measures. For example, you might add a column to the right of the criteria and rate each category using a Likert scale of 1–5, with 1 being "needs improvement," and 5 being "exemplary."

---

Summary of Standards

**Clear goals**
Does the scholar state the basic purpose of his or her work clearly?
Does the scholar define objectives that are realistic and achievable? Does the scholar identify important questions in the field?

**Adequate Preparation**
Does the scholar show an understanding of existing scholarship in the field?
Does the scholar bring the necessary skills to his or her work?
Does the scholar bring together the resources necessary to move the project forward?

**Appropriate Methods**
Does the scholar use methods appropriate to the goals?
Does the scholar apply effectively the methods selected?
Does the scholar modify procedures in response to changing circumstances?

**Significant Results**
Does the scholar achieve the goals?
Does the scholar's work add consequentially to the field?
Does the scholar's work open additional areas for further exploration?

**Effective Presentation**
Does the scholar use a suitable style and effective organization to present his or her work?
Does the scholar use appropriate forums for communicating the work to its intended audiences?
Does the scholar present his or her message with clarity and integrity?

**Reflective Critique**
Does the scholar critically evaluate his or her own work?
Does the scholar bring an appropriate breadth of evidence to his or her critique? Does the scholar use evaluation to improve the quality of future work?

---

*Figure 6.1* Assessment of Scholarship
*Source:* Adapted from Glassick et al.(1997)

Self-reflection of scholarly work is a significant part of the faculty portfolio you will build for promotion and/or tenure (Seldin & Miller, 2009). Self-reflection demonstrates strategic planning, articulates the methodology of your work, and provides an explanation of your research and supporting documentation. Self-reflection on scholarship may include why we focus on a certain topic in our discipline and why we focus on certain populations (Seldin & Miller, 2009). Overall, it provides a general method to reflect on scholarly work. The readers of your self-reflective narrative will be looking for signs of development and promise, so you will want to document a clear description of your scholarly evolution.

## Peer Feedback

Scholars can gain great feedback from peers or other outside sources. However, soliciting feedback can be intimidating. Have your peers review your CV. Or, if you are bold, move out of your comfort zone and strive for a top-tier publication or presentation. There are other ways to receive peer-review in addition to journals and conference reviewers. Brandon et al. (2015) presented the work of a small group of colleagues, who came together to read and comment on each other's work. The group contributed 10 manuscripts that had been rejected. Each member received an article that was not their own and dug in! Their results were impressive. After six months, "four manuscripts were accepted for publication and an additional five were in active revision" (p. 535). This challenge reinforces our suggestion of creating a writing group or finding a partner. Together you can accomplish your goals. Below, Brenda shares her publication history.

*When we sat down to brainstorm topics for this chapter, we discussed ways in which our scholarship has been assessed. This led to stories of our own publication history. I remember sharing how perplexed I was when one of my colleagues shared her manuscript acceptance by a top-tier journal. How is a top-tier journal defined? This led me down a rabbit trail of impact factor and journal quartile, which I still find confusing. And, don't get me started on h-index, a metric used to measure my work using the number of publications I have and how many times my work has been cited. Now, to be clear, I have a lot of respect for folks who know these things inside out. But for me, it was just too math driven. But I understood the importance of publishing in a variety of journals with a range of acceptance rates.*

*To find the information I wanted, I used Cabells, which I mentioned in Chapter 4. Cabells provides specific information about a journal. There is a lot of information, but I tend to focus on acceptance rates, how often the journal publishes each year, time from submission to publication, and any fees. I also spend time reading through the topics and disciplines to see if my work is a good fit. This way, once I have successfully published in the journal, I am able to document the metrics important to my institution. With this information, I can also be intentional with my submissions. For example, if I was published in a journal with a 40%*

acceptance rate, I will pursue a journal with a lower acceptance rate to show both the range and highlight the quality of my work.

The same can be said of conferences. Unfortunately, it is much harder to learn acceptance rates before you submit. In this instance, I chose the organization that is the best fit for my discipline. Last year, I was accepted at an international conference. When the acceptance letter arrived, it actually shared the acceptance rate. I was then able to share this information in my promotion and tenure portfolio.

When I first began submitting manuscripts to journals, I was intimidated by the process. I wanted to be successful and I knew that the more feedback I received, the stronger I would become as an author. For that reason, one of the first journals I submitted to was one that had a less than 5% acceptance rate. Now, I knew this was more than a long shot! But I strategically made this decision because I would receive five reviews. When the decision came back as a reject, I was not surprised, but the feedback was outstanding! I poured over their comments and made major changes. My manuscript was so much stronger as a result. I then submitted to a journal with a less than 15% acceptance rate and was published.

## Reviewer Feedback

The peer-review process for publication is interesting, especially in journals with low acceptance rates. We want to take this opportunity to discuss the infamous "Reviewer 2." Perhaps you have had your own experiences with Reviewer 2. There are memes dedicated to Reviewer 2 and even social media accounts dedicated to Reviewer 2. Reviewer 2's legendary reputation reflects a grouchy peer who is quick to criticize without providing helpful information or suggestions to improve the work. A quick internet search of Reviewer 2 comments yielded this post to an online platform:

> So, I got an R&R on an article from a rather well-regarded journal. While the other 2 reviewers have been constructive, reviewer 2 has been reviewer 2. They haven't bothered to be invested in what I am trying to do and have raised all kinds of tangential issues without being of any substantial help. They have also declared that my paper is "poorly conceptualized".

This is not the first time I have received harsh comments. I am just frankly upset because this review has nitpicked on random things and has not bothered to give me any helpful suggestions or directions I could pursue. I am in two minds about writing to the editor about such kinds of reviews. I have been writing and publishing for a while, so I can call the bluff. But if this review had come to me 7–8 years before, it would have really crushed me. What if this person is writing reviews for Ph.D. students or Early Career scholars and breaking their confidence? I of course don't want to be cheeky or snarky in my review responses, but I do want to share what I think with the editor. (https://www.reddit.com/r/academia/comments/14cld94/so_i_finally_had_my_reviewer_2_experienceand_i_am/)

One blogger called Reviewer 2 "the embodiment of all that is wrong with the peer-review system." They go on to share strategies to not become this kind of reviewer (https://amlbrown.com/2015/11/10/how-not-to-be-reviewer-2/). What we would like you to know is that while feedback is great, not all feedback is equal!

## SELF-MENTORSHIP

The multi-pronged approach we presented in this chapter provides a way forward to track and evaluate our scholarly activities. As you develop skills to establish a research agenda, tracking goals, growth, and progress will be essential. By examining our work, we are able to ensure academic rigor, support our own continuous improvement and therefore, professional growth. Although there are many ways to receive feedback, the goal is to seek feedback from a range of voices from various areas of expertise to strengthen your work and your ability as a writer. This chapter presented a structured approach for tracking productivity like presentations, publications, and grants. If Dr. Williams was to record her work and any metrics associated with it, she would gain a clear understanding of how effectively her work has been disseminated to and received by the public. Upon considering next steps, perhaps she will find it is time to submit to a journal with a lower acceptance rate to show both quality and quantity.

Self-mentorship can aid in scholarship assessment as you critically evaluate your own work through a reflective lens; therefore, tracking and reviewing your work on a regular basis is important. In the Mentoring Moments exercises (Exercises 4.1-4.3), we encourage you to create your own tracking template. We provide an example but encourage you to customize the template to meet your needs and goals. Next, we offer an outline of sample activities and experiences to add to your CV. Last, we encourage you to create a profile on a research platform such as Google Scholar, ResearchGate, or ResearchRabbit. These exercises offer you opportunities to showcase your work and engage with other scholars. Once you have a solid method of tracking scholarship, analyze your work using the methods you learned about in this chapter, using self-reflection and peer feedback.

## REFERENCES

Boyer, E. L. (1990). *Scholarship reconsidered: Priorities of the professoriate.* Princeton University Press, 3175 Princeton Pike, Lawrenceville, NJ 08648.

Brandon, C., Jamadar, D., Girish, G., Dong, Q., Morag, Y., & Mullan, P. (2015). Peer support of a faculty "writers' circle" increases confidence and productivity in generating scholarship. *Academic radiology, 22*(4), 534–538.

Brent, R., & Felder, R. (2016). New faculty members may not know how to teach, but at least they know how to do research… right?. *Chemical Engineering Education, 50*(4), 251–252.

Elmore, S. A., & Weston, E. H. (2020). Predatory journals: What they are and how to avoid them. *Toxicol Pathology, 48*(4), 607–610. https://pmc.ncbi.nlm.nih.gov/articles/PMC7237319/

Glassick, C. E., Huber, M. T., & Maeroff, G. I. (1997). *Scholarship assessed: Evaluation of the professoriate.* John Wiley & Sons.

Lie, J., Wilkinson, C. E., Liu, X, Wang, M., & Cao, X. E. (2024). Revising "quantity" and "quality" of science from young scholars. *ScienceDirect, 3*(6), 715–717. https://www.sciencedirect.com/science/article/abs/pii/S2590238523005787

Sahel, J. (2012). Quality versus quantity: Assessing individual research performance. *Science Translational Medicine, 3*(84). https://www.science.org/doi/10.1126/scitranslmed.3002249

Seldin, P., & Miller, J. E. (2009). *The academic portfolio: A practical guide to documenting teaching, research, and service.* Jossey-Bass.

# Section 2:
# Research and Scholarship

## CHAPTER 4: EXERCISE 4.1
### Scholarship Brainstorm

Find a quiet place where you can work without interruption. Consider the scholarship types and models presented in this chapter. Deeply consider each and how you might engage in that type of scholarship. Complete the grid below by noting ideas you have for each type of scholarship and then identifying what you need to be able to launch your scholarship.

| Scholarship Type | Idea(s) | What Do I Need to Be Able to Start? |
|---|---|---|
| Discovery | | |
| Integration | | |
| Application | | |
| Teaching | | |
| Community-Engaged | | |
| Public | | |

## CHAPTER 4: EXERCISE 4.2
## Other Scholarly Activities

There is a plethora of ways to engage in scholarly activities. Use the information provided in this chapter to brainstorm ideas you have to engage in this way. We provided two ideas to get you started and left the rest of the worksheet open for your own ideas. We include a column for "cost" as quite often the activities we wish to engage in have a dollar amount attached, and university funding is limited. Noting what the cost is for activities will help inform your decisions.

| Activity | Notes | Cost |
|---|---|---|
| Professional Organization Membership | | |
| Conference(s) | | |
| | | |
| | | |
| | | |

## CHAPTER 4: EXERCISE 4.3

### University Support for Scholarship

We encourage you to familiarize yourself with the institutional support available to you at your university. As mentioned in the chapter, many universities have an office for faculty development or have a person who focuses on faculty development on campus. Use the space below to identify the resources and support offered and note the contact person or office for each of those resources.

| University Support for Scholarship | Notes | Contact |
|---|---|---|
| | | |
| | | |
| | | |
| | | |
| | | |

## CHAPTER 5: EXERCISE 5.1
## Self-Assessment

Use this space to assess your preparation and readiness to engage in scholarship. We provided several prompts to get you started.

## Preparation:

"In reviewing my recent professional development, I feel prepared to engage in scholarship because…"

"The skills and knowledge I have developed in [specific area] prepare me to contribute to scholarly work by…"

"Reflecting on my academic background and prior experiences, I believe I am equipped to begin scholarly activities, particularly in areas such as…"

"My understanding of research methodologies and scholarship standards equips me to engage in scholarly work because…"

### Readiness to engage in scholarship

"I feel ready to engage in scholarship at this time because…"

"My current professional responsibilities and time management skills position me well for contributing to scholarship by…"

"Given my recent projects and goals, I feel ready to initiate or contribute to scholarly activities, especially in the area of…"

"The support and resources available to me have enhanced my readiness for scholarship, particularly in…"

## CHAPTER 5: EXERCISE 5.2
### Academic Mission Statement

Read Cathy Mazak's blog post "Writing an Academic Mission Statement is the first step to finding focus and taking control of your career" here: https://scholarsvoice.org/academic-mission-statement/ and then use her template below to craft your own mission statement.

**Template**

I use [methodologies/theoretical frames] to study [population] [phenomenon] [context] in order to [change you want to see in the world].

## CHAPTER 5: EXERCISE 5.3
## Goal Setting

Setting your scholarship goals is an important step to your productivity. Use the prompts below to set your goals.

1. *Reflecting on my professional growth and aspirations, my primary goals for engaging in scholarship this year are...*

2. *To achieve these goals, I plan to develop my skills in [specific areas, e.g., research methodologies, data analysis, academic writing, etc.] and seek support/resources from [e.g., colleagues, workshops, professional networks].*

3. *By setting these goals, I hope to contribute to my field by...*

4. *My first steps will be to... and I will measure my progress by...*

## CHAPTER 5: EXERCISE 5.4

### Semester Plan

The National Center for Faculty Development and Diversity (https://ncfdd.org) created a planning tool titled "Every Semester Needs a Plan". We adapted this to help with long-range planning leading to semester goals. Here is how we use the document:

1. Start with a brainstorm of research and writing you wish to engage in this semester.
2. Then do the same with scholarly activities you want to participate in.
3. Now, identify your professional goals for the semester.
4. Next, organize the activities into the chart.
5. Last, break your goals into manageable tasks you can work on each week during the semester. We begin with an example and then provide you with a chart for your own work.

**Fall / Spring / Summer                              Year**

### Research and Writing Brainstorm

**Research Project: Ideas:**

1. Profile of high school students who dropout prior to graduation
2. Bachelors's degree attainment for students with a history of foster care

**Writing Ideas:**

1. Educators and mental health partnership
2. Self-reliance of youth with foster care history
3. Mental health of youth with a history of foster care

**Ideas for Other Scholarly Activities:**

1. Join American Educational Research Association (AERA)
2. Find and join special interest groups within AERA
3. Submit a conference proposal to AERA
4. Sign-up to be a peer-reviewer for Journal of Child and Adolescent Trauma

**Professional Goals:**

1. Write 200 words twice a week August–December
2. Submit a manuscript by December 15
3. Join AERA and a special interest group
4. Submit a conference proposal
5. Sign up to be a peer-reviewer

**Create your own:**

**Semester Plan:** _____, _____
          Fall / Spring / Summer          Year

### Research and Writing Brainstorm

Research Project: Ideas:

1.
2.
3.

Writing Ideas:

1.
2.
3.

Ideas for Other Scholarly Activities :

1.
2.
3.

# EXAMPLE: Professional Goals:

## Research and Writing Deadline Calendar

| | Topic / Theme | Author(s) | Theoretical Framework | Journal Identified | Max Word Count | Due Date | Completed |
|---|---|---|---|---|---|---|---|
| 1 | Engagement | Me | | Nat'l Dropout Newsletter | 500 | September 1 | September 1 |
| 2 | Help / Survivor / Self-Reliance | Me | Emerging Adulthood | Child Welfare Journal<br>Child & Youth Services Review | 6,000 | November 1 | November 1 |
| 3 | Foster Youth – PTSD, Anxiety, Depression & Trauma | Me | Trauma and Resilience Theory | Child Abuse & Neglect | 5,000 | July 15 | July 1 |
| 4 | Trauma-Informed School Partnership with Mental Health Practitioners | Me and Co-Author | Trauma and Recovery | Journal of Child and Adolescent Trauma | 5,000 | November 1 | October 30 |
| 5 | Trauma-Informed and Professional Development with Coast School District | Co-Author and Me | | Information Age Book Publishers – Chapter Submission | 500 for proposal | February 1 | January 30 |
| 6 | High School Dropout Interviews | Me | | Northwest Journal of Teacher Educators | 5,000 | June 1 | In progress |

# Create Your Own: Professional Goals:

*Research and Writing Deadline Calendar*

| | Topic / Theme | Author(s) | Theoretical Framework | Journal Identified | Max Word Count | Due Date | Completed |
|---|---|---|---|---|---|---|---|
| 1 | | | | | | | |
| 2 | | | | | | | |
| 3 | | | | | | | |
| 4 | | | | | | | |
| 5 | | | | | | | |
| 6 | | | | | | | |

## EXAMPLE: 16-Week Semester Calendar

| Month | Date | Writing/Research Tasks | Progress / Other Notes |
|---|---|---|---|
| Aug. | Week 1 | 1. Write 333 words twice this week<br>2. Work on Nat'l Dropout Project<br>3. Write 500-word article for newsletter | |
| Aug & Sept. | Week 2 | 1. Write 333 words this week<br>2. Work on Nat'l Dropout Project<br>3. Write IRB for teachers & ACEs<br>4. Create a Google form for survey to my format | |

## Create Your Own: 16-Week Semester Calendar

| Month | Date | Writing/Research Tasks | Progress / Other Notes |
|---|---|---|---|
| Aug. | Week 1 | | |
| Aug & Sept | Week 2 | | |
| Sept. | Week 3 | | |
| Sept. | Week 4 | | |
| Sept. | Week 5 | | |
| Sept. | Week 6 | | |
| Oct. | Week 7 | | |

| Month | Date | Writing/Research Tasks | Progress / Other Notes |
|---|---|---|---|
| Oct. | Week 8 | | |
| Oct. | Week 9 | | |
| Oct. | Week 10 | | |
| Oct. & Nov. | Week 11 | | |
| Nov. | Week 12 | | |
| Nov. | Week 13 | | |
| Nov. | Week 14 | | |
| Nov. | Week 15 | | |
| Dec. | Week 16 | | |

## CHAPTER 5: EXERCISE 5.5

### Create a Writing Group

For this exercise, we offer a guide to creating a writing group, which was informed by Phillips (2014).

1. What is your goal for creating a writing group?

2. Do you want to stay within your own college or department, or include folks from across disciplines? (Strategically invite colleagues who are committed to scholarship and share similar goals.) Consider holding an "interest meeting" to gauge potential participants and clarify the group's purpose.

Once you have your group established, here are some suggested guidelines for managing your group:

1. Define the Group's Purpose and Goals:
   a. Clearly outline the purpose of the group, such as completing specific writing projects, improving writing skills, or publishing research.
   b. Set individual and group goals, breaking larger projects into manageable tasks.

2. Establish the Meeting Frequency and Duration:
   a. Decide how often to meet (e.g., 4 hours once a month or 90 minutes twice a month).
   b. Set a consistent meeting duration, allowing enough time for focused writing, discussion, and feedback.

3. Set the Group's Longevity:
   a. Choose whether the group will be semester-based, year-long, or multi-year, depending on participants' goals and commitment.

4. Choose a Meeting Location:
   a. Select a consistent and accessible location, whether it's a quiet space on campus, a library, or a virtual platform like Zoom.

5. Appoint a Group Leader:
   a. Assign a dedicated leader responsible for organizing meetings, keeping track of group goals, and maintaining the group's ideals and continuity (Philips, 2014).

6. Set Up Routines for Each Meeting:
   a. Establish a structure for each session. For example:
      - Start with goal-setting or check-ins.
      - Write for a set period.
      - End with reflections, feedback, or updates on progress.

7. Celebrate Milestones and Successes:
   a. Recognize achievements, both big and small, to keep morale high. Consider small celebrations, such as acknowledging publication acceptances or completing major project milestones.

8. Determine and Address Needs:
   a. Identify resources or support that members need (e.g., research tools, feedback, accountability) and integrate them into group activities.

9. Share Resources:
   a. Compile shared resources, such as journals, articles, writing tools, or templates, which group members can access.

10. Collaborate with Institutional Librarians:
    a. Partner with a librarian to assist with research, access to scholarly resources, or training on databases and research tools.

11. Schedule Regular Check-Ins and Adjustments:
    a. Periodically reassess the group's goals, routines, and structure to ensure they are still meeting participants' needs and adapt as necessary.

## CHAPTER 6: EXERCISE 6.1

### Journals and Manuscript Submission

For this exercise, we encourage you to use Cabells to gather important information on journals before you submit your manuscript. Once you choose your journal and submit your manuscript, record it in this tracking sheet.

| Journal Name | Impact Factor | Acceptance Rate % | Publisher | Submission Deadline | Time from Submission to Notification | Notes |
|---|---|---|---|---|---|---|
| | | | | | | |
| | | | | | | |
| | | | | | | |
| | | | | | | |
| | | | | | | |

# CHAPTER 6: EXERCISE 6.2
## Academic Scholarship Tracking & Self-Assessment Rubric

**Instructions:**

1. **Tracking**: Use this to record your scholarly activities.
2. **Self-Assessment**: Rate each category (1 = Needs Improvement, 2 = Developing, 3 = Proficient, 4 = Exemplary).
3. **Reflection**: Identify areas for growth and set goals.

### 1. Research Productivity

| Activity | Tracking | Self-Assessment (1-4) | Notes/Next Steps |
|---|---|---|---|
| Peer-Reviewed Journal Articles | # Published, Submitted | | |
| Books/Book Chapters | # Published, In Progress | | |
| Conference Presentations | # Presented, Accepted | | |
| Research Grants & Funding | # Applied, Awarded, Amount | | |

### 2. Citation Metrics & Impact

| Metric | Tracking | Self-Assessment (1-4) | Notes/Next Steps |
|---|---|---|---|
| Google Scholar Citations | # Citations, h-index, i10-index | | |
| Web of Science/Scopus Citations | # Citations, Impact Factor | | |
| Altmetrics (Social Media, Downloads) | Mentions, Shares, Downloads | | |

### 3. Contribution to the Field

| Activity | Tracking | Self-Assessment (1-4) | Notes/Next Steps |
|---|---|---|---|
| Editorial Board Roles | Journal, Years Served | | |

| Activity | Tracking | Self-Assessment (1-4) | Notes/Next Steps |
|---|---|---|---|
| Peer-Review Service | # Reviews, Journals Reviewed for | | |
| Keynote/Invited Talks | Conference, Year | | |

## 4. Collaboration & Interdisciplinary Work

| Activity | Tracking | Self-Assessment (1-4) | Notes/Next Steps |
|---|---|---|---|
| Co-Authored Publications | #, Collaborators | | |
| Interdisciplinary Research Projects | Fields, Team Members | | |

## 5. Teaching & Mentorship in Scholarship

| Activity | Tracking | Self-Assessment (1-4) | Notes/Next Steps |
|---|---|---|---|
| Student Research Supervision | # Grad/Undergrad Students | | |
| Integration of Research into Teaching | Course, Project | | |

## 6. Societal & Institutional Impact

| Activity | Tracking | Self-Assessment (1-4) | Notes/Next Steps |
|---|---|---|---|
| Public Scholarship (Op-eds, Media) | Articles, Podcasts, Interviews | | |
| Community Partnerships | Projects, Collaborators | | |

## 7. Alignment with Institutional Expectations

| Activity | Tracking | Self-Assessment (1-4) | Notes/Next Steps |
|---|---|---|---|
| Tenure & Promotion Progress | Milestones Met, Deadlines | | |

| Activity | Tracking | Self-Assessment (1-4) | Notes/Next Steps |
|---|---|---|---|
| Annual Faculty Reviews | Strengths, Areas for Growth | | |

## Reflection & Goal-Setting:

- What are your strengths?




- Which areas need improvement?




- What are your short-term (1 year) and long-term (5 years) goals?

## CHAPTER 6: EXERCISE 6.3
### Scholarly Products

Use this simple template to identify presentations, papers written during your doctoral program, your dissertation that has yet to be published.

| Product | *How do you want to turn this into a manuscript, conference proposal, or other scholarly product?* | Next Steps |
|---|---|---|
| | | |
| | | |
| | | |
| | | |
| | | |

## CHAPTER 6: EXERCISE 6.4
## Creating Your Curriculum Vitae (CV)

A curriculum vitae (CV) for university faculty is a comprehensive document highlighting your academic achievements, professional experiences, teaching, research, and service. Once you get your template set, you will want to update it often. It is easy to forget about an activity. You can also use it to track your submissions. As soon as I submit an article, I add an entry into my CV showing that the article has been submitted and is under peer-review.

There are many ways to construct your CV. For this activity we consulted several online resources. We found this AI generated format to be straight forward and inclusive of faculty activities. Using the information below, construct a CV template.

### General Formatting Guidelines

- Length: Unlike a resume, a CV has no length restriction. However, ensure clarity and relevance.
- Font and Size: Use professional fonts like Times New Roman, Arial, or Calibri in 10–12 point size.
- Margins: 1-inch margins are standard.
- Structure: Use clear headings and subheadings. Incorporate bullet points for lists.
- Order: Organize content in reverse chronological order within sections.
- Consistency: Use consistent formatting for dates, titles, and bullet points.

### Sections to Include
A. Personal Information

- Full Name
- Academic Title/Rank (e.g., Assistant Professor, Associate Professor)
- Department and University Affiliation
- Contact Information (university email, phone, and office address)

B. Education

- List all degrees earned:
    - Degree (e.g., Ph.D., M.A., B.Sc.)
    - Field of Study
    - Institution Name
    - Graduation Date (Month/Year)

C. Academic Appointments

- Positions held (e.g., Lecturer, Assistant Professor):
  - Title
  - Institution
  - Dates of Employment
  - Brief description of responsibilities (optional)

D. Research

- Publications:
  - Use citation style appropriate to your field (e.g., APA, MLA, Chicago).
  - Include peer-reviewed articles, book chapters, books, and conference proceedings.

- Grants and Funding:
  - Funding body, title, amount, and duration.

- Research Interests or Projects:
  - Briefly describe current research focus.

- Awards and Honors for Research.

E. Teaching

- Courses Taught:
  - Course name, level (e.g., undergraduate, graduate), and semester/year.

- Teaching Philosophy (optional):
  - Short statement summarizing your teaching approach.

- Curriculum Development:
  - Mention new courses or innovative teaching methods.

- Awards and Recognitions for Teaching.

F. Service

- University Service:
  - Committees, administrative roles, mentorship.

- Professional Service:
  - Editorial boards, peer-review activities, conference organizing roles.

- Community Service:
  - Outreach and public engagement relevant to your field.

G. Professional Development

- Conferences and Workshops Attended or Presented.
- Certifications and Specialized Training.

H. Additional Sections

- Professional Memberships: List memberships in academic or professional organizations.
- Languages: Indicate proficiency (if relevant).
- Technical Skills: Highlight relevant software or laboratory skills.
- References: Optionally include "Available upon request" or provide full details.

**Tips for a Strong CV**

- Tailor for Purpose: Focus on the position you're applying for; emphasize relevant teaching, research, or service.
- Keep It Updated: Regularly add new publications, presentations, and roles.
- Use Action Verbs: For example, "Developed," "Published," "Supervised," "Coordinated."
- Proofread: Ensure there are no typos or inconsistencies.

## CHAPTER 6: EXERCISE 6.5
### Promoting Your Scholarship

There are many ways for you to promote your scholarship. We present three that are free, for your consideration;

> **Google Scholar Profile:** Creating a profile allows you to add your published research. Google Scholar tracks your citations and gives you the ability to follow other researchers. You can receive notifications when those you follow have new publications, keeping you up-to-date on the latest research in your field or on your topic.

> **Research Gate:** Similar to Google Scholar, you can create a profile and add projects and publications. However, it is also a social networking platform where you can interact with others. You are able to share copies of your work with other researchers, just make sure you are following the copyright rules of your journal. ResearchGate tracks the number of people who have read your work and offers you the ability to message other scholars within the platform.

> **Research Rabbit:** Is a way to find articles and to receive curated literature recommendations based on your search history. You can add your publications and then explore the work of others on the same topic. You can also connect the literature you find to Zotero for easy collection and organization.

For this exercise, we ask you to explore all three. Create an account with one.

# Part III
# Thriving in Academia

# Chapter 7
# University and Professional Service

## FACULTY FOCUS

Dr. Carter is a first-year assistant professor in the Department of Education at a mid-sized university. With a background in K-12 literacy education, Dr. Carter is excited about her teaching and research responsibilities. However, during her annual review meeting with her department chair, she receives feedback that she should begin engaging with service activities to contribute to the university community and support her tenure track. Dr. Carter has heard colleagues mention service but isn't sure what kinds of activities count or how much time she should devote to service without compromising her research and teaching.

## INTRODUCTION

Mahatma Gandhi observed, "The best way to find yourself is to lose yourself in the service of others." Even though evaluations of faculty performance include university service, serving others is an act of kindness and compassion and typically done by servants without reward. In reality, we participate in service as teachers and scholars. Teaching is a service we provide to our students, and scholarship is the service we provide to our discipline or to our society (Buller, 2010). How do faculty members document service to their professional roles as a university professor and a scholar?

At most institutions, service refers to work outside the classroom that does not result in publication. New faculty members may be overwhelmed or tempted to only participate in required job-related activities. Even though service may not be as highly evaluated as teaching or research, service-oriented activities could benefit faculty members in many positive ways. Faculty engagement with the wider community, committees, professional organizations, or initiatives all contribute to the overall well-being and advancement of the institution and allow individuals to develop leadership skills, build networks, and positively impact their field (Irish, 2021). In this chapter, we describe service in the academic community, sometimes referred to as academic citizenship (Buller, 2010). In our description, we distinguish between university service and professional service by defining each type and outlining strategies to align service activities with your personal goals.

## WHAT IS UNIVERSITY SERVICE?

University service is the service we provide to our department, school or college, institution, or the larger community. Departmental service is a great way for you to contribute to the success of your academic unit. Sometimes serving is mandatory, while at other times it may be voluntary (Hettiarachchy, 2021). For example, advising students in your college or department is a *mandatory* part of a faculty member's job at our university. A *voluntary* example of service at the department level would be mentoring a colleague or volunteering for a committee role. Other examples of service at the department level include recruiting, organizing student events, developing curriculum, or contributing to a program review. Service at a Christian university may also include mission work. University service on a broader scale might include participation in faculty senate, chairing a committee, serving as an active sponsor or advisor for a student organization, leading a special, university wide project or initiative, recruiting, presenting at a campus-wide lecture, or volunteering at student development events (pancake suppers, move-in day).

Some university-wide committees require representation across all colleges, meaning a committee member from each college would represent their unit. For example, an awards committee or a promotion and tenure committee would be representative in order to ensure each unit has a voice. Some possible committees you might get involved with could include but are not limited to the following: Curriculum Committee, Scholarship Committee, Elections Committee, Department Research Committee, Faculty Resource Committee, Master's Committee, Doctoral Committee, Evaluation Committee.

Service outside your institution, external service, may involve community organizations (Bakken, 2011). Community service includes outreach initiatives, partnerships with local organizations, and service-learning integration. Faculty volunteer opportunities for the community might include running a clinic or center to help the public and hosting public presentations or seminars. University service encompasses public scholarship which involves sharing academic research and teaching with the public. Public scholarship bridges the gap between scholarly expertise and the public, it addresses social problems, and contributes to the public good (Motala, 2015; Northeastern University, 2025). One type of public scholarship, research-oriented public scholarship, promotes accessibility to non-academic audiences (Bold.org, 2024). For example, faculty might write articles for popular media, create educational content, or engage in public speaking. Another type of public scholarship, community-engaged scholarship, focuses on collaboration with community members or organizations on research to gain knowledge that directly benefits the community (Bold.org, 2024).

Technological advances have revolutionized the dissemination of information (Bold.org, 2025). Social media platforms provide avenues for sharing knowledge with the public. In addition, video conferencing platforms, like Zoom and Microsoft Teams, prompt communication and collaboration on a global level. Interactive webinars were widely used for common good during the COVID-19 pandemic in which global quarantines occurred. Stay at home mandates disrupted learning across all disciplines, and experts used technology tools to provide professional development. Professors Nell Duke and Pamela Mason at the University of Michigan participated in a free virtual panel discussion on the Science of Reading in November 2020. Musicians, scientists, and scholars around the globe hosted online public scholarship promoting important skills. For example, French horn player Andrew Bane of the Colborn School of Music hosted free warmups and talks on Zoom about how to be a financially stable musician. Neil deGrasse Tyson, a famous astrophysicist, hosted videos and talks on YouTube. Technology has transformed the way faculty engage in professional service, enabling collaboration and participation on a broader, more impactful scale.

## WHAT IS PROFESSIONAL SERVICE?

Professional service includes ways college professors contribute to their disciplines. Although joining professional organizations and attending and presenting at conferences are common ways to get involved in a discipline, participation beyond the basics is beneficial. At some institutions, this involvement may fall under "professional attainment" rather than service. Our faculty evaluation, which assesses service, professional attainment (scholarship), and teaching effectiveness, includes items such as *service as an officer in a professional organization* or *chairing or organizing a session or conference* in the professional attainment category rather than in the service category. Other examples of professional service include serving as an editor of a journal or as a peer-reviewer. We also realize that professional service varies from one discipline to the next. Table 7.1 presents examples of ways faculty in varying disciplines might serve their professions.

*Table 7.1* Professional Service Examples

| Discipline | Example |
| --- | --- |
| Art | **Exhibitions** - curate or participate in gallery shows to showcase work.<br>**Critiques and Reviews** - serve as jurors for art exhibitions; write reviews for publications.<br>**Event Organization:** - organize or host masterclasses for students and the public. |
| Music | **Performance** - perform at concerts, festivals, or other professional events.<br>**Adjudication** - serve as adjudicators for competitions. |
| STEM faculty | **Research** - collaborate on research efforts, serving on grant review panels, or contributing to scientific advisory boards. |
| Education | **Policy** - engage in policy advocacy, or serve on boards of educational organizations. |
| Business | **Consultation** - consult for companies, serve on corporate boards, or mentor student entrepreneurial projects. |
| All Disciplines | **Editorial and Peer-Review** - editing journals, reviewing manuscripts, or participating in professional award committees. |

We believe that getting involved in your discipline is an invaluable part of academic citizenship. This process requires some research and networking. We will describe how to "plan" for university and professional service in the next section.

## PLANNING FOR SERVICE

While service fosters leadership, it demands careful and intentional planning. Consider the level of commitment you are ready to take on. For instance, new faculty members should avoid chairing committees early in their careers and instead evaluate service opportunities thoughtfully. There are many opportunities to serve and it is easy to fill your time with meaningful activities. In your first year, you need time to get settled and find your footing. Taking on additional responsibilities often results in faculty with a strong history of teaching and service, but little time for scholarship.

## THE BASICS

Upon starting a new position, review institutional guidelines to familiarize yourself with expectations for service at departmental, college, and university level (Gasman, 2021). Check policies related to promotion and tenure that outline the importance of service contributions. Start small with minor service obligations, gradually increasing involvement over time. Consider the time and effort required, as service responsibilities are in addition to your teaching and research duties. Departmental service is a key level of involvement expected from faculty members. Speak with your department chair, dean, or faculty mentor to understand the specific service opportunities available and how they align with institutional priorities. Serving well leads to more work (Gasman, 2021). In other words, when you do a good job, you will be asked to serve more often. We do not mention this to deter you from doing a good job but to warn you that you may need to learn to say "no" to keep from being overwhelmed.

When service opportunities arise, it is essential to carefully evaluate them. Seek guidance from a faculty mentor or department chair to better understand the work performed by different committees, their meeting schedules, and the overall time commitment involved. This insight will help you make informed decisions about your participation. Be mindful that leadership positions on committees can be time-intensive, potentially distracting from teaching and research. For instance, serving as a committee chair requires familiarity with the institution's policies, processes, and culture, which new faculty may still be acquiring.

Community service requires time to build connections and relationships. This means that you will probably not be involved in much external service your first year. However, this will change once you get established with community organizations in your community or nearby communities. Building relationships in the community is essential. You may find service opportunities in community organizations as a volunteer (i.e., helping out with the community organization on an as-needed basis), through special events (i.e., helping out with a fundraiser), as a board member (i.e., more of a time commitment helping the organization move forward), or even a board officer (i.e., extreme time commitment working with the growth and development of the organization). Prior to relocating to Texas, Brenda served the Department of Human Services Foster Care division in various capacities for several years. It began with an introduction after a presentation on foster care and educational needs and turned into an invitation to connect with others from the department, which became a request to chair a committee. This year, she joined a committee at the Texas Department of Human Services, which supports families and youth transitioning out of foster care. This group has experts from various backgrounds and represents different segments of the community. It has been a great way to serve and to network. No doubt, there will be additional opportunities that will come from this group. Our advice is to start out small, possibly as a volunteer, as an initial step in becoming involved with a community organization. It also provides you with the opportunity to determine if this organization is a good match for you and your interests and skills.

Planning for professional service requires you to first be familiar with local, state, national, and international organizations that align with your area of expertise. For example, Jodi is a literacy educator and enjoys participation in state (Texas Association of Literacy Education), national (Association of Literacy Educators and Researchers), and international (International Literacy Association and the Literacy Research Association) organizations. Determine which organizations provide a means to stay updated on the latest research and trends in your field. Seek organizations that offer professional development, leadership opportunities, and platforms, like conferences, to present research and to enhance your academic reputation. Organizations you find and enjoy will provide networking and collaboration opportunities at the very least. It is important to find your people in order to know how you might want to serve your profession!

## BEYOND THE BASICS

Some volunteer leadership positions in higher education entail opportunities to shape academic policies and contribute meaningfully to an institution's success. For example, academic council (faculty senate, faculty council) is the primary governing body to recommend the educational policy of the university and advise the president on its implementation, and provides for faculty, staff, and student participation in academic governance. The group of peer-elected leaders fosters collaboration across all academic units and advocates for faculty needs. Effective leaders are needed to ensure that the council operates efficiently. This type of work is intense and is considered "beyond the basics" because it is leadership within service and requires a larger time commitment than other university committees.

Contributing to a university's strategic plan or participating in a major initiative is another impactful way to support and enhance your institution's success. After completing her first year, Brenda was approached by the provost with a request to write a Quality Enhancement Plan (QEP) for the university over the summer. As a new faculty member, I didn't know what a QEP was, let alone what it entailed. Thankfully, I was provided with a template and took it from there. It was a large undertaking, but it was an honor to be asked and a great opportunity to engage with senior-level administration.

The same is true of professional service—some volunteer leadership positions provide opportunities to shape policies and contribute meaningfully to the advancement of your discipline. Once you get involved at a basic level of participation in professional organizations, you may consider leadership opportunities. Attend board meetings to learn about the culture and needs of the organization, follow the organization's social media posts to identify opportunities, and visit with peers to discuss ways to get involved. Since organizations vary in size, it may beneficial to share your skills with smaller organizations at the local or state level. Volunteering may take the form of committee work or peer-reviewing conference proposals. More time-consuming positions may include service as an officer of the governing board or working with the conference organization committee. In addition, editorial work for academic journals, consultation, advocacy, and possibly development may become avenues for faculty to make a difference.

## SELF-MENTORSHIP

Service can support your teaching, scholarship, and professional development. This chapter addressed academic citizenship in the form of university and professional service and as a way for faculty to develop leadership skills, build networks, and positively impact their field.

When considering service opportunities, regardless of the type, we encourage you to be thoughtful and intentional. As discussed in this chapter, there are several forms of service and various places for you to contribute. Start small and evaluate opportunities carefully.

Self-mentorship allows you to proactively identify areas to which to devote your time and energy. Therefore, conduct do your research as you seek relevant service opportunities. Critically reflect on your potential contributions. Our Mentoring Moments exercises (Exercises 7.1-7.3) will have you consider how your service could inform your research, how your research could lead to service, and how it can contribute to your tenure and promotion. Set goals and manage your time so that you have a balance between teaching, research, and service.

## REFERENCES

Bakken, J. P., & Simpson, C. G. (2011). *A survival guide for new faculty members: Outlining the keys to success for promotion and tenure.* Charles C. Thomas.

Bold.org (June 2, 2024). The rise of public scholarship. Scholarship Blog. https://bold.org/blog/the-rise-of-public-scholarship/

Buller, J. L. (2010). *The essential college professor: A practical guide to an academic career.* Jossey-Bass.

Gasman, M. (2021). *Candid advice for new faculty members: A guide to getting tenure and advancing your academic career.* Myers Education Press.

Hettiarachchy, J. (2021). *A survival guide for college and university professors.* GoToPublish.

Irish, A. (2021). How to get more out of service. *Inside Higher Education.* https://www.insidehighered.com/advice/2021/08/03/how-use-service-bolster-your-academic-career-opinion

Motala, E. (2015). Public scholarship, democracy and scholarship engagement. *Educational Research for Social Change,* 4(2), 22–34. https://lsa.umich.edu/content/dam/ncid-assets/ncid-documents/Ten%20Diversity%20Scholarship%20Resources/Motala%20(2015)%20Public%20Scholarship%2C%20Democracy%2C%20and%20Scholarly%20Engagement%20%20(1).pdf

Northeastern University (2025). About public scholarship. The Ethics Institute. https://cssh.northeastern.edu/ethics/about-public-scholarship/

Chapter 8

# Faculty Evaluation

**FACULTY FOCUS**

*Case Study 1: Dr. Knudson*

Dr. Knudson joined the Department of Education at a mid-sized research university as an assistant professor in 2019. With a specialization in special education, she entered the tenure track with a clear understanding of the university's tenure expectations in teaching, scholarship, and service. Early on, she initiated a strategic plan to ensure a successful tenure and promotion process. During her first semester, she familiarized herself with the university's tenure guidelines and consulted with senior faculty and administrators to determine their expectations. She sought clarity on the standards for research publications, teaching effectiveness, and service contributions.

Committed to quality instruction, Dr. Knudson implemented innovative teaching strategies, including technology integration and community-based learning projects. She consistently received positive student evaluations and invited peers to observe her teaching to provide feedback. She also mentored doctoral students, co-authoring research papers with them to enhance their professional development.

Dr. Knudson set a goal of publishing at least two peer-reviewed journal articles per year, focusing on high-impact journals in special education. She also pursued external grant funding, securing a $50,000 grant in her third year to support her research on adaptive technologies in K-12 settings. Additionally, she presented at state and national conferences, including the Council for Exceptional Children (CEC) Convention, to increase the visibility of her work on special education trends.

Dr. Knudson took on meaningful service roles within her department and professional organizations. She chaired the curriculum committee, leading revisions to the special education program. Additionally, she coordinated community events to support the local special education population.

Throughout her tenure journey, Dr. Knudson regularly met with her assigned faculty mentor and sought feedback on her progress. She also underwent annual *performance reviews and used the feedback to strengthen her research, teaching, and service contributions. In her fifth year, Dr. Knudson prepared her tenure portfolio, which included a comprehensive record of her achievements. External reviewers—leaders in the field of literacy education—provided strong letters of support, highlighting the significance of her research contributions. In her sixth year, she successfully received tenure and was promoted to Associate Professor.*

## Case Study 2: Dr. Alan Rose-Barrio

*Dr. Rose-Barrio joined the Department of Humanities as an assistant professor of English in 2018. With a specialization in American Literature, Dr. Rose-Barrio entered the tenure track with enthusiasm but without a solid plan to meet the university's expectations for tenure and promotion. Over the years, various challenges hindered a successful tenure outcome.*

*Despite initial orientation sessions and faculty handbooks outlining tenure requirements, Dr. Rose-Barrio remained uncertain about the necessary benchmarks for teaching, scholarship, and service and did not take proactive steps to clarify expectations with senior faculty or the department chair.*

*While Dr. Rose-Barrio was knowledgeable in American Literature, student evaluations were mostly negative and inconsistent. He neglected to address feedback from course evaluations and did not participate in faculty development workshops. As a result, he could not provide evidence of teaching effectiveness.*

*Dr. Rose-Barrio struggled to find time to write and publish and submitted just one article for publication, falling below the department's expectations. Additionally, there was minimal effort to participate in professional organizations or secure internal or external funding.*

*Dr. Rose-Barrio took on a few service roles in his department, but he did not actively engage in university committees or leadership roles. Unlike colleagues who sought mentorship, Dr. Rose-Barrio did not regularly consult with senior faculty for guidance. Annual performance reviews emphasized areas for improvement, but little action was taken to address these concerns.*

*In the sixth year, Dr. Rose-Barrio submitted his tenure portfolio. However, the promotion and tenure committee provided mixed feedback, citing a lack of growth in teaching effectiveness and insufficient scholarly attainment. Departmental colleagues were also hesitant to provide strong letters of support due to concerns about teaching effectiveness and service. As a result, the tenure application was denied, and Dr. Rose-Barrio faced a terminal year contract.*

## INTRODUCTION

The tenure process is a rigorous process, in which you must achieve rigorous standards in the areas of teaching, scholarship, and service. Chapters 1–7 framed success in the way of planning, engaging and assessing. Now that you have reached the chapter on faculty evaluation, you have the tools needed to connect the pieces/components of academia, teaching effectiveness, scholarship, and service, to build a portfolio for your academic career. From the annual evaluations to tenure and promotion opportunities, faculty members must curate evidence of growth and success in these three categories.

Up until this chapter, our Faculty Focus scenarios have described the experiences of new faculty members. In this chapter, we present case studies of faculty early in their tenure appointments. The rationale for this shift in focus aligns with the purpose of this chapter, which is to provide guidelines to support new faculty's understanding of tenure and promotion expectations, including annual evaluation processes and the development of a strong and comprehensive faculty portfolio. The case studies describe one professor who has successfully planned for tenure and promotion and one who has not. We build on these examples to demonstrate the impact planning, assessment, and self-reflection have on your applications for promotion and tenure.

## FACULTY EVALUATION

Dr. Knudson's preparation for tenure reflects rigor and planning. She started planning early, establishing clear goals and timelines for teaching, research, and service. She implemented evidence-based and innovative classroom practices, clearly documenting student success and feedback. She engaged with senior colleagues and solicited feedback regularly. She also maintained a steady publication record and sought funding opportunities. On the other hand, Dr. Rose-Barrio experienced challenges, which stemmed from a lack of strategic planning. He was unclear about institutional expectations and missed necessary benchmarks for teaching, research, and service. Dr. Rose-Barrio exhibited strong content but struggled to demonstrate effective teaching. His scholarly production was limited, and he did not actively engage in departmental service or professional development, or consult with senior faculty for guidance. Overall, his challenges began with a lack of knowledge about tenure and promotion expectations at his university.

### Understand Institutional Expectations

The tenure and promotion process varies from one institution to the next. Large tier one universities have rigorous research standards, while smaller universities with an emphasis on teaching and learning have less rigorous expectations. Understanding institutional standards is key to success. One major consideration is the weighing of the categories. At our university, teaching effectiveness makes up 60% of our annual evaluation, and university service and scholarship are each worth 20%.

In addition to considering the weighing of categories, ask questions about evaluation criteria. For example, inquire about the specific research expectations, like the number of publications expected annually. Ask your dean, associate dean, department chair, or any other administrators and colleagues about their perspectives on scholarly production. Explore the CVs of colleagues who were recently awarded tenure. Examine the quantity and quality of the articles they published, considering the author order and the impact of the journals they published in (Gasman, 2021). Identify the types of service they document along with their presentations, grant activity, and other discipline-related efforts.

## THE BASICS

Documenting growth and development is a part of the evaluation process. As we mentioned in Chapter 6, growth and development depends on the tracking and assessment of your work. This extends to all categories of faculty expectations, including teaching, scholarship and service. Dr. Rose-Barrio was not only unprepared, the Promotion and Tenure committee may have concerns about his growth during his time at the university. There are procedures in place to prevent this from happening. First of all, annual faculty evaluations provide a structured way to assess a faculty member's performance, typically in the categories of teaching, research, and service. The process also allows for feedback, professional development, identification of areas for improvement, and informed decision-making regarding promotion and tenure. In addition, most universities have a pre-tenure review in place to support faculty like Dr. Rose-Barrio, who may not be ready for review. The pre-tenure review is a formal evaluation process, which precedes the formal review in order to provide feedback on the progress toward tenure.

### Sample Portfolio Guidelines

Again, universities differ in their evaluation techniques. In this section, we use a general set of guidelines as an example of how you might support your tenure or promotion application and provide narratives to support your attainment of teaching effectiveness, scholarship, and university service. We also include a section on *collegiality*, which is considered a priority at our university.

### Teaching Effectiveness

To demonstrate teaching effectiveness, you may be asked to provide narratives about your philosophy of teaching, the instructional methods that constitute best practices in your discipline, teaching responsibilities, curricular revisions, teaching innovations or efforts taken to improve teaching, and evaluation of your teaching (student, peer, faculty, etc.). Share attendance at teaching improvement conferences (when; where), how you are applying what you learned, any evidence of growth or change in your teaching, how you have responded when students make suggestions for change, and steps you have taken to improve teaching. In addition to written narratives, be prepared to provide all student and faculty evaluations as links or appendices. Identify specific excerpts from evaluations you can use in your narratives that tie in with our philosophy or teaching ethos, including any changes you made based on analysis and reflection of evaluations. Include sample comments from evaluations as well as student emails and letters. As members of a Christian university, we also include our integration of faith with our discipline.

## Scholarship

Your narratives on scholarly production (professional attainment) should be written so that anyone outside of your discipline can understand your achievements. You should provide evidence (in an appendix, for instance) for any items mentioned. For example, if your CV includes conference presentations, share artifacts like conference programs or presentation slides. Some people even share photos from the conference.

Narratives in this category might focus on research and scholarship, professional memberships and offices held (overlaps with professional service), grant work, collaborative projects, conference participation, awards and scholarships, and supervision of student research. Include examples of your publications (books, articles, and/or creative works), describing the significance of the work and its importance to your discipline. Statements from others may also support the significance of your work.

## Service

Your narrative regarding university service should include selective samples of your contributions to committees within and outside your department. Documentation may also cover your role in advising, mentorship, service-learning activities, and sponsoring student organizations. Your narrative should include your leadership on campus. What are noteworthy ways in which you have served the faculty, students and the community? Include your time commitments. For example, share any offices held or special tasks you were given. Documentation of service activities may include agendas, minutes, programs, or certificates/awards for service.

Letters of recommendation from colleagues provide additional support for these three evaluation categories. The university will collect letters from your supervisors and other tenured faculty. We recommend you solicit letters from colleagues and peers who can attest to your teaching, research, or service.

## Collegiality

Our university considers collegiality to be a way of conducting oneself in a respectful and dignified way toward each member of our learning community, in order to promote the good of the university. Collegial faculty get along with others, collaborate, and share responsibility. Collegiality is important because it fosters a positive work culture.

## BEYOND THE BASICS

Constructing a portfolio takes time. Locating and saving all the necessary documentation can be a challenge. There are a couple of ways to plan for this. One way is to have a drawer or file dedicated to your conference acceptances, handwritten thank you notes from colleagues and students, course evaluations, etc. In addition to a physical file, you will have many artifacts that you have received or accessed electronically. Regardless of how you choose to keep these items, we have the following recommendations: 1. Create a folder on your desktop labeled "tenure and promotion"; when those artifacts arrive electronically or in hardcopy, move them to this folder; 2. For hardcopy items, simply scan and add to the folder. At the end of each semester, go through your tracking forms to cross-reference your activities with the artifacts you have. 3. Make a list of what, if anything, is missing. 4. Download and archive your course evaluations. 5. If you want to be uberorganized, add sub-folders for teaching, research, and service.

## The Faculty Portfolio

Our university provides faculty with an outline of what is required for the portfolio, including guidelines for word count for each narrative. Figure 8.1 presents one example of how we organized our portfolio and a sample of what was included:

*Faculty Evaluations—UMHB*
**Evaluation 2021**

- Signed Faculty Evaluation 2021.pdf

**Evaluation 2022**

- Signed Faculty Evaluation 2022.pdf

**Teaching Effectiveness Plans**

- Teaching Effectiveness Plan 2022.pdf

- Teaching Effectiveness Plan - Evaluation 2022.docx
- Teaching Effectiveness Plan 2023.docx

## Faculty Evaluations—Previous Institution (Promotion & Tenure Documentation)

- Tenure Review 2015.doc
- Faculty Growth Plans 2009–2021.docx
- Dean's Report—- Sixth Year Faculty Review.pdf
- Personnel Committee Letter of Support for Tenure.pdf
- Sixth Year Faculty Review.pdf
- Third Year Faculty Review.pdf

## Samples of Syllabi

- Syllabus, EDUC-7301-01, Fall 2022.pdf
- Syllabus, EDAD-6364, Spring 2023.pdf
- Syllabus, EDAD-6364, Spring 2023.pdf
- Syllabus, EDUC-4328, Spring 2023.pdf
- Syllabus, EDUC-7303, Summer 2023.pdf
- Syllabus, EDUC-7301, Fall 2023.pdf
- Syllabus, EDUC-6352, Fall 2023.pdf
- Syllabus, EDUC-3341, Fall 2023.pdf

## Curriculum Vitae

- Morton, CV

## Graduate Faculty Scholarship Activity

- Graduate Faculty Scholarship Summary 2021.docx
- Graduate Faculty Scholarship Summary 2022.docx
- Graduate Faculty Scholarship Summary 2023.docx

## Research & Scholarship Documents

- Course at UT.pdf
- Publication Summary.docx

## Invited Presentations & Keynotes
*Invited and Peer-Reviewed Conference Presentations Summary.docx*
- Invited Keynote and Training—John Brown University.pdf

- Invited Presentation at Baylor—Thank you.pdf
- Baylor Letter to Dr. Berry.pdf
- Invited Presentation—Corban University.docx
- Invited Research Presentation at ACU.pdf
- Keynote Address—Casper College, 2020.pdf
- UofT Conference Abstract.docx

*Awards / Scholarships*

- Alumni Magazine Article on Trauma work in Estonia.pdf
- Assoc for Childhood Education International Award.pdf
- Morton Fulbright Grant.pdf
- Morton, Brenda_Estonia (1).pdf
- Fulbright Specialist Completion Certificate (2).pdf
- Fulbright Specialist Program Certificate.pdf
- Grantee Press Release_Morton.pdf

*Grants / Proposals Written, Funded*

- Morton, B. Fulbright Project Statement.pdf
- Fulbright Specialist Project—Approved.docx
- UMHB Graduate Faculty Research Proposal—Funded, 2022.pdf

*Selected Samples of Conference Presentations*

- 2022 Creating Trauma Sensitive Schools Conference Presentations.pdf
- ATE Conference Presentations, 2022.pdf
- ISPCAN Conference Certificate.pdf

*Student Advising, Mentoring Junior Colleagues, Service Learning*

- Master's thesis Signature Page.pdf
- U of Tartu Master's Thesis Advisor.pdf
- Bates Honor College Thesis Advisor.pdf

*Selected Samples of Service to UMHB and the Greater Community*

- Scholars Day 2023 Faculty Sponsorship.pdf
- Scholars Day 2022 Faculty Sponsorship.pdf
- ACU Research Presentation.pdf
- CELT Presentation 2022.pdf
- COE 2023–24 Study Abroad Proposal.docx

- Fall Faculty Workshop 22–5.pdf
- Fulbright Selection Committee.pdf
- Invited Presentation Corban University.docx
- Invited Research Presentation at ACU.pdf Links to an External Site.
- Scholars Day 2022 Thank You Note.pdf Links to an External Site.
- Scholars Day 2022 Faculty Sponsorship.pdf Links to an External Site.
- Thank You for Serving on the Fulbright National Screening Committee.eml
- U of Tartu Estonia Contribution Award.pdf

*Additional Professional Development*

- AERA Research Professional Development Course May 2022.pdf
- CELT Participation 2021.pdf
- CELT Participation 2022.pdf
- ISPCAN International Webinar Series Certificate of Attendance. Multidisciplinary Collaboration in Child Protection (1).pdf
- ISPCAN Webinar Certificate of Attendance. Protecting Children from Maltreatment Across All Ages in Challenging Times.pdf
- ISPCAN Webinar Professional Development August 2022.pdf
- Polyvagal Professional Development.pdf

*Letters of Support*

- Univ of Tartu Letter of Support.docx
- UMHB Alumni Letter of Support.docx
- Colleague Letter of Support.pdf
- UMHB Alumni Letter of Support.pdf
- Current Student Letter of Support.pdf
- Colleague from Former Institution Letter of Support.pdf
- Tallinn Univ Letter of Support.pdf
- Colleague Letter of Support.pdf

*Selected Student Notes*

- Email from Student 1.docx
- Email from Student 2.eml
- Email from Student 3.eml
- Email from Student 4.eml
- Email from Student 5.eml
- Student Thank you Note 1.pdf
- Student Thank you Note 2.pdf

- Student Thank you Note 3.pdf
- Student Thank you Note 4.pdf
- Student Thank you Note 5.pdf

### Administration & Faculty Notes

- Note from President.pdf
- Note from Provost.pdf
- Scholars Day 2022 Thank you Note.pdf
- Thank you Note for Scholars Day Support.pdf
- Thank you Note from Dean.pdf

### Service-Learning Tallinn University, Estonia

- TLU LIFE project—A Child with a Different Emotional Experience in the Camp—Innovation that Integrates Disciplines.pdf

## SELF-MENTORSHIP

Tenure is not the end. As covered in the previous chapters, great teaching is informed by research, and both teaching and research create continued opportunities to serve your university and communities. Once you have your portfolio created, continue to add and reflect on your work. At the end of each year, complete an analysis of all you accomplished and where you dedicated your time. Post-tenure is also a time to mentor junior faculty. Model life-long learning. Remember what it was like, in these moments, to be the new faculty member and extend an invitation to support them in ways you were supported and mentored.

## REFERENCE

Gasman, M. (2021). *Candid advice for new faculty members: A guide to getting tenure and advancing your academic career*. Myers Education Press.

Chapter 9

# Thriving in Academia

## FACULTY FOCUS

*Dr. Mitchell is a tenured full professor in the Mathematics department. He was finishing his lecture to a group of students when a female student appeared to be experiencing emotional distress. Before he could finish his lecture, the student burst into tears and fled the classroom. Dr. Mitchell cut his lecture short and quickly ran down the hall after the student. He found her outside the restroom, visibly distressed. She began hyperventilating and shaking. Unsure of what to do, Dr. Mitchell knew he needed help to deal with the situation. He walked the student to an administrator, who called the mental health response team to support her.*

*This was not the first time Dr. Mitchell had engaged with a student experiencing mental health issues, and it was beginning to take a toll on his own well-being. While he always wanted to be supportive and compassionate toward his students, the cumulative weight of these encounters was starting to deteriorate his own mental health. The incident left him feeling unprepared and overwhelmed, highlighting a need to better care for his own mental health while continuing to support his students, but where to start.*

## INTRODUCTION

As presented in this book, the work and expectations of university faculty are multi-faceted. Teaching, research, and service activities contribute to the promotion and tenure process. These expectations remained constant, even in light of the pandemic. During the pandemic, issues that existed prior to 2020 worsened and, in many cases, were exploited.

The pandemic brought collective trauma world-wide, impacting individuals and families (Kaubisch et al., 2022). It created financial and socioemotional stress for many families. Many businesses moved to remote work environments, if they were able. Many parents and caregivers scrambled to navigate their new reality as both employee and parent, working and parenting/supervising their children during their work day and supporting their child during online learning (Benner & Mistry, 2020). This issue was particularly impactful for women, as they historically have carried the majority of the household and caretaking tasks, more so than their male counterparts (Kantamnemi, 2020). Stress and anxiety mounted in the home as the parent or primary caregiver began to face serious challenges like housing and/or food insecurity, in the midst of few job prospects. Many lost loved ones during this time. It is no wonder that the mental health of adults and children suffered and that this continues to impact people.

As early as 2010, the mental health of students was noted as on the decline (Flaherty, 2021). As the mental health needs of students has increased, it has impacted faculty well-being, leading to an imbalance in job satisfaction. A 2022 survey conducted by Inside Higher Ed reported that 79% of provosts saw a higher-than-average turnover rate of their faculty (Flaherty, 2022). A second study conducted by *The Chronicle of Higher Education* and Fidelity Investments found 69% of faculty members reported symptoms of stress and 55% had considered early retirement or career change (Fidelity Investment and the Chronicle of Higher Education Study, 2021). A 2022–2023 study by Healthy Minds Network found 64% of faculty reported feeling burned out to some degree with more than 90% reporting "student mental health is significantly worse now than when they began their careers" impacting their own mental health and well being (Vyletel et al., 2023, para 3). What contributed to the rise in mental health issues? And, what can faculty do?

In this book, we have explored the work of faculty, considering the tasks they engage in and the pathway to tenure and promotion. One area we have yet to fully address involves the diverse needs of the students we serve and how those needs intersect with our responsibilities in teaching, research, and service. The purpose of this chapter is to explore the challenges in academia that contribute to stress and burnout among university faculty and to present sustainable self-care tools and strategies to support faculty retention.

## ACADEMIC STRESSORS

Common sources of stress for faculty include workload and time management. These encompass teaching, grading, research deadlines, and administrative tasks. Consider the experiences of faculty during the pandemic. Classes pivoted to virtual instruction, often with little or no training on virtual pedagogy. Faculty and students worked to figure things out, leaving both with a soured experience. It is no surprise that during and immediately following the COVID-19 pandemic there was a large turnover in faculty nationwide. It has become common for faculty members to be the first person a student approaches to share their struggle with mental health. "Professors have to navigate the boundary between being a supportive advisor while also maintaining the firm line of being a professor; this boundary navigation can be challenging and emotional" (Chazan-Gabbard, 2023, p. 1). Through no fault of their own, students are struggling and in many cases are seeking help and support.

Chessman (2023) wrote an article that was published in the online journal *Higher Education Today*, in which she addresses the issue of faculty burnout head-on. Chessman notes that while mandates and isolation practices from the COVID-19 pandemic are gone, faculty burnout remains high. Professional burnout is a psychological condition that adversely affects an individual's connection to their work, leading to emotional exhaustion, diminished job engagement, reduced commitment, and, at times, unprofessional behavior in the workplace (Rakovec-Felser, 2011). One reason for burnout is the excessive work load of university faculty, which has a negative impact on faculty members' wellbeing (Xu & Wang, 2023). In addition to a larger work load, faculty are also engaging with a generation of students experiencing heightened mental health challenges, which requires an expanded role and skill set to provide adequate support.

A study conducted by Boston University School of Public Health, the Mary Christie Foundation, and the Healthy Minds Network in early 2021 explored how the work of faculty related to the mental health of their students. The survey received 1,685 responses from faculty members representing 12 colleges/universities across the United States. The purpose of the survey was to gather data on faculty's perceptions and experiences with student mental health needs and the support both students and faculty needed. There were several key findings, including data showing that 87% of respondents believed that the mental health of their students had declined during the COVID-19 pandemic. Second, approximately 80% of faculty shared they had conversations with students about their mental health. When asked if they felt they were able to recognize if a student was in emotional or mental distress, only 51% said yes. When asked about their own mental health as faculty members, 21% shared that supporting student mental health had a negative impact on their own mental health. Last, the majority of participants reported welcoming professional development on student mental health if their institution was to offer this training. This study illuminates the need for training and support, and recognizes that faculty are encountering significant student needs, which are impacting their own wellbeing. As professors work to address these evolving needs, often without extensive mental health training, they can experience significant distress and emotional burnout, which highlights the urgent need for effective self-care practices.

## SELF-CARE

At the beginning of a new semester, a colleague from another institution joined a scheduled meeting. It was evident he was clearly under the weather. He shared that he had purchased a townhome and moved in, moved his office to the new location his institution had assigned to him, and traveled to see family. He then laughed and shared that as a mental health provider, he knew the importance of caring for himself, in particular during periods of high stress. Yet, he did not do it. His body determined enough was enough and he was forced to take a break.

Professors are very aware of student needs and are looking for a way to support their students, while also managing the tasks they are responsible for (Lipson, 2021; Price et al., 2020). The term "self-care" has gained mainstream popularity over the last decade. It has been defined by many reputable organizations, including The National Institute of Mental Health (NIMH) and The World Health Organization (WHO). The WHO defines self-care as "the ability of individuals, families, and communities to promote health, prevent disease, maintain health, and cope with illness and disability with or without the support of a healthcare provider" (https://www.who.int/news-room/fact-sheets/detail/self-care-health-interventions). The NIMH says "self-care means taking the time to do things that help you live well and improve both your physical health and mental health" (https://www.nimh.nih.gov/health/topics/caring-for-your-mental-health). Regardless of what organization you choose, self-care is a wholistic approach to engaging in practices that improve physical and mental health.

The idea of caring for one's self is not a new concept, but has been proposed as a way for helping professionals to take care of themselves while caring for others. Given the very nature of those in the helping field, the idea that your own psychological well-being could be impacted by hearing the stories of others resonated with folks and gave a name to what people were experiencing. Pearlam & Saakvitne (1995) and Figley (2002) were some of the first to talk about this idea of re-traumatization and/or compassion fatigue as professional hazards of helping professionals. It is also appropriate to apply this concept to educators, yet until a few years ago, this language was not included in educational training or conversations. I (Brenda) became familiar with their work while enrolled in a post-doc in trauma response. I remember reading their work and the work of others, then engaging in a conversation with my professor, a mental health professional. I remember sharing that compassion fatigue accurately describes what many educators were experiencing, yet they didn't know this was the cause. As this concept and language began to seep into the literature to describe the experiences of educators, it slowly became a part of our own shared language. However, it was not clear how to combat re-traumatization or compassion fatigue, and people were only hearing about the idea of self-care.

The number of domains of self-care varies according to the model chosen, with some proposing five, six, and even eight domains. And within each of these, there are variations on what those five, six, and eight are. We chose the work of Butler et al. (2019), who proposed six domains. Their work is unique in that they added "relationship" to their list of domains. The six include: physical, professional, relational, emotional, psychological, and spiritual self-care. They described each domain as follows:

## Physical

This domain is defined as "tending to the needs of the physical body in order to achieve or support optimal functioning and to avoid breakdowns or deteriorations within systems" (p.109). The authors go on to discuss the importance of sleep, nutrition, exercise, and health maintenance.

## Professional

This domain focuses on managing or preventing "work-related stress and stressors, reduce the risk or mitigate the effects of burnout and other workplace hazards, and increase work performance and satisfaction" (p. 110–111). This includes job stress and burnout, job engagement, secondary traumatic stress and re-traumatization, occupational hazards, and compassion satisfaction.

## Relational

This domain refers to the "efforts we make to maintain and enhance our interpersonal connection to others" (p. 112). Categories included in this domain are social integration and social support, altruism, and virtual social networks.

## Emotional

This domain is defined as "practices that are engaged in to safeguard against or address negative emotional experience as well as those intended to create or enhance positive emotional experience and well-being" (p. 114). In this domain, the authors challenge readers to consider identifying and replacing destructive ways of coping, reducing negative emotional experience, and increasing well-being and happiness.

## Psychological

The authors describe this domain as having two purposes. They are "pursuing and satisfying intellectual needs and purposeful and reflective efforts to understand and attend to the overall needs of the organism" (p. 116). Here, they encourage intellectual pursuits and other enjoyable activities of the mind and self-awareness and mindful reflection on self.

## Spiritual

This domain focuses on faith-based spirituality, including religious participation and prayer, and secular or non-faith-based spirituality, through spiritual meditation and connection with nature. The authors define this domain as one that "creates space to reflect on our own inner needs and our role or place within the world and universe" (p. 117).

As mentioned, we purposefully chose the work of Butler et al. (2019). Their inclusion of relationships felt like a holistic approach to self-care. Garbett & Thomas (2020) expanded on the role of friendships in academia. The two developed a deep friendship despite the physical distance. Dr. Garbett is from New Zealand and Dr. Thomas from Canada. They began as two colleagues comparing teacher education programs, but that was moved to the periphery as they found similarities in their struggles in both their personal and professional lives. They launched a self-study. What they found was that inter-collegial friendships were "crucial to being able to live well within the academy" (p. 296).

While their findings are not surprising, I (Brenda) had not considered how my close friends in the academy have positively contributed to my own self-care until I read Garbett and Thomas (2020). Reading Garbett and Thomas' study and learning more about their relationship was inspiring. Both of us have inter-collegial friendships that are very important to us. Yes, I love my friends and spending time with them brings joy, but I had not realised that by being in community with each other, I was caring for myself and for my friends. We know our relationships have been significant to our own wellbeing. We encourage you to find your person or your people!

Using these six domains and definitions, we move to the practice of self-care. But before we do, we need to address misunderstandings of self-care. First, because of the dearth of information you can find on self-care, there can be the belief that self-care is simply self-indulgence. However, this is far from the truth. Self-indulgence focuses on immediate gratification without considering long-term consequences. While binge-watching your favorite show might offer short-term enjoyment, it's hard to argue that it contributes to your physical well-being. By contrast, spending an hour connecting with a friend or hiking a trail has clear connections to psychological and physical health. Second, creating space for self-care can also feel counterproductive. Feeling the pressure of looming deadlines and grading can make it difficult to keep an appointment with yourself to engage in self-care. Yet, keeping that lunch appointment with a friend or meeting for a quick walk through campus is important. Prioritizing engagement in the six domains can provide the energy and bandwidth to complete tasks.

## SELF-CARE STRATEGIES FOR FACULTY

A simple internet search for self-care strategies or self-care practices yields a plethora of results. Here we provide a short list of ideas for strategies and practices you can engage in on your self-care journey.

- Time Management and Boundaries:
  - Setting Boundaries: Strategies for establishing work/life boundaries, including saying "no" and setting clear communication limits with students and colleagues.
  - Effective Time Management: Tips for prioritizing tasks, organizing work, and using tools like time-blocking or the Pomodoro technique.
  - Breaks: Importance of taking time off, even if it's micro-breaks during the workday.

- Physical Health:
  - Exercise and Movement: Incorporating physical activity throughout the day, even with a busy schedule.
  - Sleep Hygiene: Practical ways to improve sleep quality, including setting a routine and reducing screen time.
  - Nutrition Tips: Quick, healthy eating tips tailored to the academic lifestyle.
  - Mental and Emotional Well-Being:
  - Mindfulness and Meditation: Simple exercises to practice mindfulness, even between classes or meetings.
  - Journaling and Reflection: How reflective writing can help process academic experiences and reduce stress.
  - Professional Support: Encouraging use of counseling services, mentorship, and peer support for emotional and mental health.

- Social and Relational Self-Care:
  - Collegial Support: Fostering community within departments and with peers at other institutions.
  - Work-Life Balance: Ways to maintain relationships outside of work and avoid isolation.
  - Mentorship: Benefits of being both a mentor and a mentee to foster professional relationships and gain support.

## IMPLEMENTING YOUR SELF-CARE PLAN

In the subsequent Mentoring Moments pages, you will have an opportunity to create your own self-care plan. The task is not too difficult, but sticking to it could prove to be a bit harder. As you create your plan, we encourage you to think about sustainability and flexibility. Keep the following in mind:

**Goals:** Set personalized, achievable goals for your self-care practices. Perhaps you want to pack a healthy lunch the night before so that you can ensure a balanced meal, or you want to take a walk through your neighborhood before you get to work. Whatever it is, remember, it takes time for a new routine or practice to become a habit. Celebrate when you achieve those goals, and be kind to yourself when you fall a bit short of the goals you set.

**Routine:** Setting a routine is recommended to protect the time for your self-care practice. You might consider booking time with yourself on your calendar, just as we suggested for scholarship endeavors. Find places in your day where you can spend 10 or 15 minutes engaging with your colleagues, getting some fresh air by walking around campus, or spending time meditating.

**Partners:** Finding a colleague or friend helps to stay consistent with self-care goals. You can share a self-care strategy together, or simply check in with one another to see how your practice went that week. Determine what is best for you and then find your people.

**Reflection:** We encourage you to regularly reflect on how your practice is going. Are the goals you set and the routine you created working for you?

**Adjust:** After working through your personal reflection, evaluate what if anything needs to be adjusted. Perhaps that meditation appointment on Wednesday at 3:00 pm is consistently being interrupted by a committee meeting. Adjust the time, the day, or the place if that will help you be successful.

**Resources/Support:** Take a moment to create a list of off- and on-campus resources that support your goals and routine. Perhaps it is taking advantage of your university workout center or attending a workshop on wellness programs. Explore what is available to you to help you on your journey.

## THE BASICS

Let's revisit Dr. Mitchell from the beginning of this chapter. Dr. Mitchell could use a self-care plan! Our hope would be that he would create a plan and stick with it. Even small changes and practices can make a world of difference. Dr. Mitchell could consider a small step, like connecting with a friend at least once a week for a short catch-up session. This is a practice I (Brenda) have found particularly enjoyable. I am on one side of campus and my friend is in the middle of campus. We found an easy meeting place, where we connect and then do a short walking loop to enjoy fresh air. Our time together may only be 10–15 minutes, but it brings joy and a welcome break.

## BEYOND THE BASICS

In the Mentoring Moments exercises, we encourage you to complete the Pro-QOL survey to evaluate where you are with compassion fatigue, compassion satisfaction, and burnout. This survey is free and you can take it as many times as you would like. Another measure is the Maslach Burnout Inventory, which is a self-reported questionnaire that assesses the thoughts of individuals on their work activity. It considers three dimensions: "emotional exhaustion, depersonalization, and reduced personal accomplishment" (Fernández-Suárez et al., 2021, p. 1). This tool offers several variations with one specific to educators. The tool is fee based.

## SELF-MENTORING

Whether practicing self-care is new to you or an old friend that has sustained you, we hope we have encouraged you to prioritize self-care. As faculty mentors, we hope you will pay attention to signs that exhaustion or burnout could be around the corner if you don't do something now. Academia is a fantastic place to spend your career. We want to set you up for longevity in the profession and experience success and joy along the way. Remember, self-care is not self-indulgence, but rather your sustainability plan.

Let's revisit Dr. Mitchell and the experience he went through with a student. We are grateful for the empathy and care he showed his student and for knowing the resources that could support her that were on campus. We also acknowledge that this can be emotionally exhausting and, depending on your own struggles, it can hit close to home. It is crucial that you care for yourself so that you can continue to care for others. In the Mentoring Moments, you will be encouraged to reflect on your own well-being in Exercises 9.1 and 9.2. We provide you with guidance and suggestions to create care plans to sustain you so that you can continue to grow and thrive in academia.

## REFERENCES

Benner, A. D., & Mistry, R. S. (2020). Child development during the COVID-19 pandemic through a life course theory lens. *Child development perspectives*, 14(4), 236–243.

Butler, L. D., Mercer, K. A., McClain-Meeder, K., Horne, D. M., & Dudley, M. (2019). Six domains of self-care: Attending to the whole person. *Journal of Human Behavior in the Social Environment*, 29(1), 107–124. https://doi.org/10.1080/10911359.2018.1482483

Chazan-Gabbard, C. F. (2023). "100%, I'm not trained for this:" Understanding How Professors Navigate Higher Education as Student Mental Health Declines. *PANDION: The Osprey Journal of Research and Ideas*, 4(1), 12. https://digitalcommons.unf.edu/cgi/viewcontent.cgi?article=1072&context=pandion_unf

Chessman, H. M. (2023, May 18). *Effective strategies for combating faculty burnout.* Higher Education Today. https://www.higheredtoday.org/2023/05/18/effective-strategies-for-combating-faculty-burnout/

Fernández-Suárez, I., García-González, M. A., Torrano, F., & García-González, G. (2021). Study of the prevalence of burnout in university professors in the period 2005–2020. *Education Research International, 2021*(1), 7810659.

Fidelity Investments, & The Chronicle of Higher Education. (2021, February 25). *Fidelity Investments & The Chronicle of Higher Education study: More than half of college and university faculty considering leaving teaching, citing burnout caused by pandemic.* Business Wire. https://www.businesswire.com/news/home/20210225005616/en/Fidelity-Investments-The-Chronicle-of-Higher-Education-Study-More-Than-Half-of-College-and-University-Faculty-Considering-Leaving-Teaching-Citing-Burnout-Caused-by-Pandemic

Figley, C. R. (2002). Compassion fatigue: Psychotherapists' chronic lack of self care. *Journal of clinical psychology, 58*(11), 1433–1441.

Flaherty, C. (2022, July 5). *Professors are leaving academe during the great resignation.* Inside Higher Ed. https://www.insidehighered.com/news/2022/07/05/professors-are-leaving-academe-during-great-resignation

Garbett, D., & Thomas, L. (2020). Developing inter-collegial friendships to sustain professional wellbeing in the academy. *Teachers and teaching, 26*(3–4), 295–306.

Kantamneni, N. (2020). The impact of the COVID-19 pandemic on marginalized populations in the United States: A research agenda. *Journal of vocational behavior, 119*, 103439.

Kaubisch, L. T., Reck, C., & Josef Woll, C. F. (2022). The COVID-19 pandemic as a traumatic event and the associated psychological impact on families – A systematic review. *Journal of Affective Disorders, 319*, 27. https://doi.org/10.1016/j.jad.2022.08.109

Lipson, S.K. (2021). *The role of faculty in student mental health.* Boston University School of Public Health. https://marychristieinstitute.org/wp-content/uploads/2021/04/The-Role-of-Faculty-in-Student-Mental-Health.pdf

Pearlman, L. A., & Mac Ian, P. S. (1995). Vicarious Traumatization: An Empirical Study of the Effects of Trauma Work on Trauma Therapists. *Professional Psychology: Research and Practice,* 26(6), 558–565. doi:10.1037/0735–7028.26.6.558

Price, S.F., Carmack, H.J., & Kuang, K. (2020). Contradictions and predicaments in instructors' boundary negotiations of students' health disclosures. *Health Communications, 36*(7), 795–803. https://doi.org/10.1080/10410236.2020.1712525

Rakovec-Felser, A. (2011). Professional burnout as the state and process: What to do? *Coll Antropol, 35,* 577–585. https://pubmed.ncbi.nlm.nih.gov/21755734/

Vyletel, L. (2023). *Faculty burnout survey.* American Psychological Association. https://www.apa.org/ed/precollege/psychology-teacher-network/introductory-psychology/faculty-burnout-survey

Xu, Y., & Wang, Y. (2023). Job stress and university faculty members' life satisfaction: The mediating role of emotional burnout. *Frontiers in Psychology, 14,* 1111434.

# Section 3:
# Thriving in Academia

## CHAPTER 7: EXERCISE 7.1
### Partners

For this exercise, we ask you to brainstorm a list of potential partners.

| Organization | Contact Information | Ideas for a Partnership |
| --- | --- | --- |
| | | |
| | | |
| | | |
| | | |
| | | |

# CHAPTER 7: EXERCISE 7.2
## Professional Organizations

Identify professional organizations that align with your discipline. Search for membership information, upcoming conferences you might attend, ways you might get involved (do they have publications?).

| Organization | Reach International, National, State, Local | Membership Information (Cost) | Website Information | Ways to Serve |
|---|---|---|---|---|
| | | | | |
| | | | | |
| | | | | |
| | | | | |

## CHAPTER 7: EXERCISE 7.3
### Roberts Rules of Order

Service may include leadership opportunities on committees and boards in which you need to be familiar with parliamentary procedures. Review the following resources on Roberts Rules of Order. Make notes about major motions you need to know for meetings:

https://www.sa.gov/files/assets/main/v/1/ce/documents/roberts-rules-of-order.pdf

https://www.ulm.edu/staffsenate/documents/roberts-rules-of-order.pdf

https://diphi.web.unc.edu/wp-content/uploads/sites/2645/2012/02/MSG-ROBERTS_RULES_CHEAT_SHEET.pdf

### Notes

_____

_____

_____

_____

_____

_____

_____

_____

_____

## CHAPTER 8: EXERCISE 8.1

## CHAPTER 9: EXERCISE 9.1

### Assess Your Professional Quality of Life

For this exercise, go to https://proqol.org/proqol-measure. You will find the assessment as an online tool, or you can download the form and self-score. Once you have found your scores, record them here:

Compassion Satisfaction Score: _____

Burnout Score: _____

Secondary Traumatic Stress Score: _____

We encourage you to retake this assessment throughout your academic year.

## CHAPTER 9: EXERCISE 9.2

### Identify Your Self-Care Needs

In this exercise, we encourage you to identify your self-care needs. You will be prompted to consider both daily self-care and emergency self-care.

Take a moment to consider what you value and need in your everyday life (daily self-care needs) versus what you value and need in the event of a crisis (emergency self-care needs). Remember that self-care extends far beyond your basic physical needs: consider your psychological, emotional, spiritual, social, financial, and workplace well-being.

### Daily Self-Care

What are you doing to support your overall well-being on a day-to-day basis? Do you engage in self-care practices now? Are you more active in some areas of self-care than others? Use the list in the chapter of strategies to give you ideas for your daily self-care practice. You can use the table below to help you determine which areas may need more support.

| Area of Self-Care | Current Practices | Practices to Try |
|---|---|---|
| Physical (e.g. eat regular and healthy meals, good sleep habits, regular exercise, medical check-ups, etc.) | | |
| Emotional (e.g. engage in positive activities, acknowledge my own accomplishments, express emotions in a healthy way, etc.) | | |
| Spiritual (e.g. read inspirational literature, self-reflection, spend time in nature, meditate, explore spiritual connections, etc.) | | |

*(Continued)*

| Area of Self-Care | Current Practices | Practices to Try |
|---|---|---|
| **Professional** (e.g. pursue meaningful work, maintain work-life balance, positive relationships with co-workers, time management skills, etc.) | | |
| **Social** (e.g. healthy relationships, make time for family/ friends, schedule dates with partner/spouse, ask for support from family and friends, etc.) | | |
| **Financial** (e.g. understand how finances impact your quality of life, create a budget or financial plan, pay off debt, etc.) | | |
| **Psychological** (e.g. take time for yourself, disconnect from electronic devices, journal, pursue new interests, learn new skills, access psychotherapy, life coaching, or counselling support through your EFAP if needed, etc.) | | |

## Emergency Self-Care

When you are faced with a crisis, you likely won't have time to create a coping strategy. Take time to develop a plan in advance, so it's there when you need it.

We encourage you to work through the chart below and identify what is helpful and what is harmful.

| Emergency Self-Care Tools | Helpful (What to Do) | Harmful (What to Avoid) |
| --- | --- | --- |
| **Relaxation/Staying Calm** Which activities help you to relax (e.g. deep breathing, taking a walk)? Which activities make you more agitated or frustrated (e.g. yelling, swearing, or drinking)? | | |
| **Self-Talk** Helpful self-talk may include, "I am safe/I can do this." Harmful self-talk may include, "I can't handle this/I knew this would happen/I deserve this." | | |
| **Social Support** Which family members and friends can you reach out to for help or support? Which people should you avoid during times of stress? Be honest about who helps and who zaps your energy. | | |
| **Mood** Which activities support a positive mood (e.g. listening to uplifting music, enjoying the sunshine)? What should you avoid when times get tough (e.g. staying in bed all day, avoiding social activities)? | | |

*(Continued)*

| Emergency Self-Care Tools | Helpful (What to Do) | Harmful (What to Avoid) |
|---|---|---|
| **Resilience**<br>What, or who, helps you to get through difficult times? What helps you bounce back? Conversely, what or who feeds negativity for you? | | |

Adapted from https://brocku.ca/human-rights/wp-content/uploads/sites/208/unct-ye-dss-doc-building-self-care-toolkit-en.pdf

# Index

Note: **Bold** page numbers refer to tables and *italic* page numbers refer to figures.

academia: council 150; experience 1; freedom 22–23; leader 7; stressors 164–165; thriving in 10–11, 163–171
academic freedom 22–23
accommodations 43, 45–46; presentation 45; response 46; setting 46; timing/scheduling 46
accountability 50, 102
adjunct 5, 21
Adverse Childhood Experiences (ACEs) 19, 20
AI-generated assignment 54
American Association of University Professors (AAUP) 22, 49
American Educational Research Association (AERA) 87
Americans with Disabilities Act (ADA) (1990) 28, 43, 45
andragogy 34
Architectural Barriers Act (1968) 28
Arnsparger, A. 21
artificial intelligence (AI) 52, 84, 98
assessments 50; formative 51, 56; institutional 50; performance **52**; quantitative 51–52; summative 51
assistant professors 5
associate professors 5

Association for American Colleges and Universities (AACU) 24
asynchronous learning 42

Bakken, J. P. 39
Bane, Andrew 147
Belcher, Wendy: *Writing Your Journal Article in Twelve Weeks: A Guide to Academic Publishing Success* 96, 101
Berardi, A. 19
Berg, M. 78; *The Slow Professor* 78
Blaustein, M. 37
Boyer, Ernest 78, 79, 85, 108, 111, 112
Brandon, C. 113
Butler, L. D. 167, 168

Cabells 88
Carnegie Foundation for the Advancement of Teaching 42, 112
ChatGPT 98
Chessman, H. M. 165
Chronicle of Higher Education and Fidelity Investments 164
cognitive-behavioral therapy (CBT) 82
Colbeck, C. L. 85
college professor 5, 6, 8
collegiality 7, 156, 158

# INDEX

Common Core State Standards Initiative (CCSSI) 18
community: engagement 84; service 146, 149
Community-Engaged Scholarship (CES) 84–85
conference presentations 109, 157
constructive feedback 54–55
constructivism 34
content delivery 45
content knowledge (CK) 26
course: calendar 44; content 21; delivery 41–42; information 41–42; materials 43
course learning outcomes (CLOs) 41, 50
credit hours 41–42
curriculum: backward design 44, 50, 95
curriculum vitae (CV) 87, 100, 111

departmental service 146, 149
Dewey, John 22, 34, 35, 37
Director of Strategic Partnerships 86
documentation service 157
Drivalas, J. 21
Duke, Nell 147

education: capital 2–3; requirements 3, 5
effective reading program 36
Einstein, Albert 107
Elmore, S. A. 110
Enlightenment 18
Evans, L. 3
experiential learning 35, 36

faculty: portfolio 158–162; role of 77; scholarship 89
faculty evaluation 155–156; collegiality 156; scholarship 157; self-mentorship 162; service 157; teaching effectiveness 156–157; UMHB *158–162*; understand institutional expectations 155–156
Figley, C. R. 166

Fischer, K. 20
Fischman, W. 20
Five W's (Who, What, When, Where, and Why) framework 5–10
Flodén, F. 55
formative assessments 51, 56
Fulbright 103–104

Garbett, D. 168
Gardner, H. 20
Generation X 20
Generation Z (GenZ) 20
Glassick, C. E. 78, 83, 108, 112
good teachers 24
grading policies 44
grant writing 100, 110
Great Society programs 18

Harvard University 2
Henry VIII 1–2
higher education 2; student feedback in 55; teaching challenges in 18–21
*Higher Education Today* 165
Higher Learning Commission's (HLC) 5
high-impact practices (HIPs) 23–25, 88
h-index 109, 110
Homer: *The Odyssey* 3

information: course 41–42; instructor 40–41
*Inside Higher Education* 5
institutional assessment, in higher education 50
instructional course teams 39
instructor information 40–41
integration 80–81
international organizations 28, 149–150
iPads 83–84

job: educational requirements 3, 5; opportunities 8
Johnson, Lyndon 18

# INDEX

Kezar, A. 7
King, Martin Luther, Jr. 22
Kinniburgh, K. J. 37
Knowles, Malcolm 34
Kuh, George 23–25
KWL chart 11–12

land-grant colleges 78
learning: active 37; asynchronous 42; experiential 35, 36; objectives 41; student 41; synchronous 42; traditional 42
Learning Management System (LMS) 33, 45
Lehrfreiheit 22
Lernfreiheit 22
Lewis, Takeisha 77, 88, 89
Lie, J. 109
Literacy Research Association (LRA) 109
literal tracking 111
Lovejoy, Arthur 22

Mahatma Gandhi 143
Maslach Burnout Inventory 171
Mason, Pamela 147
Master of Arts (MAT) 8
Maxey, D. 7
Mazak, Cathy 93, 94, 102
McTighe, Jay 44, 50, 95
mental health 19, 20
mentor/advisor 6, 99–100
Mentoring Moments 11, 24, 29, 46, 105, 171
mentorship 3–4
Michael, P. W. 85
millennials 20
Morrill Act (1862) 78
Morton, B.M. 19

National Center for Education 19
National Institute of Mental Health (NIMH) 166
National Institutes of Health (NIH) 110

National Science Foundation (NSF) 110
Network on Education and Academic Rights (NEAR) 22
neurodevelopment 19
*New York Times* 8

O'Donnell, K. 23
*The Odyssey* (Homer) 3
Open Access (OA) materials 43
Open Educational Resources (OER) 43

pandemic 163–164
Pedagogical Content Knowledge (PCK) 26
Pedagogical Knowledge (PK) 26
pedagogy 25–26, 34
peer feedback 113–114
peer observations 57, 58
peer-review process 98–99, 109
performance assessments 52, **52**
Perry, B. D. 37
Pew Research Center 20
portfolios 53, 58
postsecondary teacher 3, 5
presentations 53, 109
Princeton Review (2025) 5
professional development (PD) 58, 103
professional service 147–148, **148**
professor 1; assistant 5; associate 5; college 5; Five W's Framework 5–10; history of 1–2; responsibility of 6–7; role of 2–3; tenure 5, 7
program learning objectives (PLOs) 41
publications 109–110
public scholarship 85–87, 146–147

Quality Enhancement Plan (QEP) 150
quantitative assessment 51–52

Rehabilitation Act (1973) 43
research: focus 92–93; schedule 95–96
Reviewer 2 99, 101, 114, 115
reviewer feedback 114–115

# INDEX

Rodriguez, Alicita 5
rubrics 36, 38, 39, 53–54
scholarship 10, 91; activities 87; activities tracking 110–111; of application 81–83; assessment 115; Brenda's story 113–114; colleagues, collaborating with 100–101; community, finding a scholarly 102–103; criteria 108; of discovery 79–80; engaging in 91, 94–99; evaluation of 108–110; expanded model of 111; faculty 89; find a mentor 99–100; goal setting 95–96; grant writing 110; historical perspective 78–79; of integration 80–81; literal tracking 111; multi-pronged approach 107–108; peer feedback 113–114; physical space 95; planning for 92–94; and professional attainment 87–88; reconsidered 79; research schedule 95–96; reviewer feedback 114–115; self-assessment *112*, 112–113; self-reflection of 113; of teaching 83–84; time 94–95
Schreyer Institute for Teaching Excellence 25
Seeber, B. K. 78; *The Slow Professor* 78
self-assessment 112–113
self-awareness 11, 46, 167
self-care 166–167; effective time management 169; emotional 167; physical 167; plan 169–170; professional 167; psychological 167; relational 167; self-mentoring 171; setting boundaries 169; social and relational 169; spiritual 168; strategies 169
self-indulgence 168
self-mentorship 11, 29, 46, 58, 89, 105, 115
self-reflection 57, 113
service: community 146, 149; departmental 146, 149; documentation 157; opportunities 149; planning for 148; professional 147–148, **148**, 150; self-mentorship 151; teaching 145; university 145–147, 157; voluntary 146
Sheri Vasinda 100, 101
Shulman, L. S. 26
Silvia, P. J. 94, 95; *Write It Up: Practical Strategies for Writing and Publishing Journal Articles* 96, 102
*The Slow Professor* (Berg and Seeber) 78
social media 100, 147
Spady, W. G. 50
student 20; engagement 24; feedback 55; focus and management 23; GenZ 20; learning 25, 41; mental health of 164; projects 53
students' evaluations of teaching (SET) 49, 55–56
summative assessments 51
Sword, H. 94
syllabus 39, 40
synchronous learning 42

teacher/practitioner 6
teaching: responsibilities 6; self-evaluation of 24; service 145
teaching effectiveness 10, 17–29; assessing 56–58; assessment 50; basics 21; course content 21–23; definitions of 17; evaluating 49–58; high-impact practices 24–25; improving 56–58; observations 57; pedagogy 25–26; portfolios 58; preparing for 33–46; professional development (PD) 58; self-reflection 57; student focus and management 23
teaching philosophy 34; Brenda 37–39; Jodi 35–37; planning 39–40
Technological, Pedagogical and Content Knowledge (TPACK) 27, *27*
Technology Camp 83
technology integration 26–28

technology knowledge (TK) 26
tenure: process 154–155, 162; professors 5; track position 9
Texas Association of Literacy Education (TALE) 109
Texas Department of Human Services 149
textbook 42–43; reading assignments 36
Thomas, L. 168
traditional learning 42
trauma 19, 37–39
two face-to-face (f2f) 33, 38

United Nations Educational, Scientific, and Cultural Organization (UNESCO) 22
United States (US): education 18; higher education 2
Universal Design for Learning 28–29
university: policies 43; service 145–147, 157

Urban Green Initiative (UGI) 85
U.S. Bureau of Labor Statistics 2

van Der Kolk, B. A. 37
Vygotsky, Lev 37

Weston, E. H. 110
Wiggins, Grant 44, 50, 95
World Health Organization (WHO) 166
*Write It Up: Practical Strategies for Writing and Publishing Journal Articles* (Silvia) 96, 102
writing: counts as 96; grant 110; group 101–102; tools 96–98, **97–98**
*Writing Your Journal Article in Twelve Weeks: A Guide to Academic Publishing Success* (Belcher) 96, 101

Yapa, L. 85
YouTube 20

For Product Safety Concerns and Information please contact our EU representative  GPSR@taylorandfrancis.com
Taylor & Francis Verlag GmbH, Kaufingerstraße 24, 80331 München, Germany

www.ingramcontent.com/pod-product-compliance
Lightning Source LLC
Chambersburg PA
CBHW051358290426
44108CB00015B/2068